OPPOSING
VIEWPOINTS®
SERIES

Community Policing

DISCARD

Other Books of Related Interest:

Opposing Viewpoints Series

American Values

Civil Liberties

Corporate Social Responsibility

Organized Crime

The Death Penalty

At Issue Series

Road Rage

Self-Defense Laws

Current Controversies Series

Family Violence

Violence in the Media

"Congress shall make
no law . . . abridging
the freedom of speech,
or of the press."

First Amendment to the US Constitution

The basic foundation of our democracy is the First Amendment guarantee of freedom of expression. The Opposing Viewpoints Series is dedicated to the concept of this basic freedom and the idea that it is more important to practice it than to enshrine it.

OPPOSING
VIEWPOINTS®
SERIES

Community Policing

Roman Espejo, Book Editor

GREENHAVEN PRESS
A part of Gale, Cengage Learning

GALE
CENGAGE Learning·

Farmington Hills, Mich • San Francisco • New York • Waterville, Maine
Meriden, Conn • Mason, Ohio • Chicago

GALE
CENGAGE Learning·

Elizabeth Des Chenes, *Director, Content Strategy*
Cynthia Sanner, *Publisher*
Douglas Dentino, *Manager, New Product*

For more information, contact:
Greenhaven Press
27500 Drake Rd.
Farmington Hills, MI 48331-3535
Or you can visit our Internet site at gale.cengage.com

For product information and technology assistance, contact us at

Gale Customer Support, 1-800-877-4253
For permission to use material from this text or product, submit all requests online at
www.cengage.com/permissions

Further permissions questions can be emailed to permissionrequest@cengage.com

Articles in Greenhaven Press anthologies are often edited for length to meet page requirements. In addition, original titles of these works are changed to clearly present the main thesis and to explicitly indicate the author's opinion. Every effort is made to ensure that Greenhaven Press accurately reflects the original intent of the authors. Every effort has been made to trace the owners of copyrighted material.

Cover image © daseaford/Shutterstock.com.

LIBRARY OF CONGRESS CATALOGING-IN-PUBLICATION DATA

Community policing (Greenhaven Press)
  Community policing / Roman Espejo, book editor.
     pages cm. -- (Opposing viewpoints)
  Includes bibliographical references and index.
  ISBN 978-0-7377-6951-7 (hardcover) -- ISBN 978-0-7377-6952-4 (pbk.)
1. Community policing--United States--Juvenile literature. I. Espejo, Roman, 1977-
II. Title.
  HV7936.C83C6596 2014
  363.2'3--dc23
                                                                          2013043018

Printed in the United States of America
1 2 3 4 5 6 7 18 17 16 15 14

Contents

Why Consider Opposing Viewpoints?   11

Introduction   14

Chapter 1: How Should Community Policing Be Implemented?

Chapter Preface   19

1. Community Policing Solves Problems   21
   in Partnership with the Community
   Victor E. Kappeler and Larry K. Gaines

2. Community Policing Is Different   28
   from Traditional Policing
   Matthew Scheider

3. Community Policing Requires the Involvement   33
   and Understanding of Communities
   Linda S. Miller, Kären Matison Hess, and
   Christine Hess Orthmann

4. Community Policing Without the Police? The   44
   Limits of Order Maintenance by the Community
   David Thacher

5. Community Policing or Homeland Security: 52
   Sophie's Choice for Police?
   Douglas Page

6. The Real Truth of Community Policing   60
   William L. Harvey

Periodical and Internet Sources Bibliography   65

Chapter 2: Are Community Policing and Neighborhood Watch Programs Effective?

Chapter Preface   67

1. Community Policing Can Be Effective   **69**
   If Properly Practiced
   Police Magazine

2. Community Policing May Not Reduce Crime   **80**
   Jeremy M. Wilson and Amy G. Cox

3. Neighborhood Watch Groups   **86**
   Do Not Increase Safety
   Jonathan Simon

4. Neighborhood Watch Groups Should   **91**
   Not Be Armed
   Michael Rubinkam

Periodical and Internet Sources Bibliography   **96**

**Chapter 3: How Can Community
Policing Be Improved?**

Chapter Preface   **98**

1. Community Policing Needs Various   **100**
   Sources of Support
   Zach Friend and Rick Martinez

2. How the Federal Government Is Killing   **109**
   Community Policing
   Sudhir Venkatesh

3. On the Block   **115**
   Chris Smith

4. Social Media Can Enhance Community Policing   **124**
   Dan Alexander

5. Community Policing Must Adapt   **132**
   to Different Communities' Needs
   John Markovic

6. Improving Police-Community Relations   **140**
   Can Improve Community Policing
   Katherine Freeman-Otte

7. Planning the Implementation   148
   of Community Policing
   Michael J. Palmiotto

Periodical and Internet Sources Bibliography   160

Chapter 4: Do Stand Your Ground Laws Empower Citizens?

Chapter Preface   162

1. The New Vigilantes: Trayvon Martin   164
   and the "Shoot First" Lobby
   Chris Kromm

2. Standing Your Ground and Vigilantism   171
   Robert VerBruggen

3. Stand Your Ground Laws Put Safety at Risk   175
   Justin Peters

4. Storming the Castle Doctrine   180
   William J. Watkins Jr.

5. The Use of Deadly Force Allowed in Stand Your   189
   Ground Laws Should Be a Last Resort
   Joshua K. Roberts

Periodical and Internet Sources Bibliography   196
For Further Discussion   197
Organizations to Contact   199
Bibliography of Books   203
Index   206

Why Consider Opposing Viewpoints?

> *"The only way in which a human being can make some approach to knowing the whole of a subject is by hearing what can be said about it by persons of every variety of opinion and studying all modes in which it can be looked at by every character of mind. No wise man ever acquired his wisdom in any mode but this."*
>
> *John Stuart Mill*

In our media-intensive culture it is not difficult to find differing opinions. Thousands of newspapers and magazines and dozens of radio and television talk shows resound with differing points of view. The difficulty lies in deciding which opinion to agree with and which "experts" seem the most credible. The more inundated we become with differing opinions and claims, the more essential it is to hone critical reading and thinking skills to evaluate these ideas. Opposing Viewpoints books address this problem directly by presenting stimulating debates that can be used to enhance and teach these skills. The varied opinions contained in each book examine many different aspects of a single issue. While examining these conveniently edited opposing views, readers can develop critical thinking skills such as the ability to compare and contrast authors' credibility, facts, argumentation styles, use of persuasive techniques, and other stylistic tools. In short, the Opposing Viewpoints Series is an ideal way to attain the higher-level thinking and reading skills so essential in a culture of diverse and contradictory opinions.

In addition to providing a tool for critical thinking, Opposing Viewpoints books challenge readers to question their own strongly held opinions and assumptions. Most people form their opinions on the basis of upbringing, peer pressure, and personal, cultural, or professional bias. By reading carefully balanced opposing views, readers must directly confront new ideas as well as the opinions of those with whom they disagree. This is not to simplistically argue that everyone who reads opposing views will—or should—change his or her opinion. Instead, the series enhances readers' understanding of their own views by encouraging confrontation with opposing ideas. Careful examination of others' views can lead to the readers' understanding of the logical inconsistencies in their own opinions, perspective on why they hold an opinion, and the consideration of the possibility that their opinion requires further evaluation.

Evaluating Other Opinions

To ensure that this type of examination occurs, Opposing Viewpoints books present all types of opinions. Prominent spokespeople on different sides of each issue as well as well-known professionals from many disciplines challenge the reader. An additional goal of the series is to provide a forum for other, less known, or even unpopular viewpoints. The opinion of an ordinary person who has had to make the decision to cut off life support from a terminally ill relative, for example, may be just as valuable and provide just as much insight as a medical ethicist's professional opinion. The editors have two additional purposes in including these less known views. One, the editors encourage readers to respect others' opinions—even when not enhanced by professional credibility. It is only by reading or listening to and objectively evaluating others' ideas that one can determine whether they are worthy of consideration. Two, the inclusion of such viewpoints encourages the important critical thinking skill of objectively evaluating an author's credentials and bias. This evaluation will illuminate an author's reasons for taking a particular stance on an issue and will aid in readers' evaluation of the author's ideas.

It is our hope that these books will give readers a deeper understanding of the issues debated and an appreciation of the complexity of even seemingly simple issues when good and honest people disagree. This awareness is particularly important in a democratic society such as ours in which people enter into public debate to determine the common good. Those with whom one disagrees should not be regarded as enemies but rather as people whose views deserve careful examination and may shed light on one's own.

Thomas Jefferson once said that "difference of opinion leads to inquiry, and inquiry to truth." Jefferson, a broadly educated man, argued that "if a nation expects to be ignorant and free ... it expects what never was and never will be." As individuals and as a nation, it is imperative that we consider the opinions of others and examine them with skill and discernment. The Opposing Viewpoints Series is intended to help readers achieve this goal.

David L. Bender and Bruno Leone,
Founders

Introduction

> *"[The Office of Community Oriented Policing Service] has been effective in putting more police officers on the street. The best available evidence suggests that more police lead to less crime."*
>
> *Jens Ludwig and John J. Donohue III, economists*

> *"Outcomes from the Community Oriented Policing Services grants call into question the assumption that more expenditures on police are the best way of keeping communities safe."*
>
> *Justice Policy Institute*

Part of the US Department of Justice (DOJ), the Office of Community Oriented Policing Services (COPS) was created by Title I of the Violent Crime Control and Law Enforcement Act. "The COPS Office was established in 1994 to assist state, local, and tribal law enforcement agencies in enhancing their effectiveness in building their capacity to advance public safety through the implementation of community policing strategies,"[1] states the DOJ. Community policing is a philosophy in which police departments and communities work in partnership to reduce crime and address social problems. The office aims to aid law enforcement through the attainment of several goals, including,

- focusing hiring grants on "neighborhood level" community policing partnerships and problem solving;

- aligning training and technical assistance in a more substantial way to officer hiring;

- continuing to promote improved public safety outcomes by infusing its core principles in all grant programs, acting on evidence that community policing advances public safety;

- continuing to support innovative programs that respond directly to the emerging needs of state, local, and tribal law enforcement in order to shift law enforcement's focus to preventing, rather than reacting to crime and disorder within their communities;

- developing, delivering, and continuing to evaluate state-of-the-art training and technical assistance to enhance law enforcement officers' problem-solving and community-interaction skills;

- promoting collaboration between law enforcement; community members; academic institutions; and other key stakeholders to develop innovative evidence-based initiatives to prevent crime.[2]

Since 1994, COPS claims to have funded more than thirteen thousand law enforcement agencies nationwide through various programs and initiatives, placing an additional 124,000 officers on the streets. For the fiscal year (FY) 2014, it requested $439.5 million, including $257 million for the COPS Hiring Program and $150 million for the Comprehensive School Safety Program, which was proposed in January 2013. The DOJ claims that the office "will maintain an outcome performance measure established in FY 2013 to assess the impact of the COPS Hiring Program funding on the crime problem of homicide."[3]

Some research supports the effectiveness of COPS funding in fighting crime. In their 2007 analysis, researchers William N. Evans and Emily G. Owens reported that the average COPS hiring grant reduced robberies by 5 percent, assaults by 3.6 percent, automobile thefts by 3.3 percent, homicides by 3.2 percent, and burglaries by 2.2 percent. According to Evans and

Owens, this funding "led to a statistically precise drop in crime in subsequent years for four of the seven index crimes."[4] Additionally, the US Government Accountability Office (GAO) estimated that the COPS hiring grants accounted for 5 percent of the 26 percent drop in crime between 1993 and 2000. The GAO also found that the hiring grants had the most positive impact on crime rates in towns and citizens with populations between 50,000 and 149,000.

Nonetheless, other researchers concluded that COPS funding marginally affects crime rates. In 2006, the Heritage Foundation's Center for Data Analysis (CDA) reported that increasing hiring grants by 1 percent was associated with a mere reduction of 0.01 percent in robbery rates. "The hiring grants' meager effect on robberies and the lack of statistically significant findings for the six other crime categories suggest that new funding for the hiring grants will do little to help large cities fight crime,"[5] asserts David B. Muhlhausen, a research fellow at CDA. Furthermore, after determining that 189 large cities receiving COPS funds saw insignificant crime reductions between 1990 and 2000, researchers John Worrall and Tom Kovandzic argued that "a strategy of throwing money at the crime problem, of simply hiring more police officers, does not seem to help reduce crime to a significant extent."[6]

The establishment of COPS was a key development in the community policing movement in the United States. As a law enforcement philosophy, its wide range of practices and strategies are intended to deepen the relationship that a police department forms with the neighborhood it serves and further engage members of the neighborhood in the mission to fight crime. Also, while distinct from community policing, neighborhood watch programs and self-defense policies are germane to the role of citizenship in crime prevention.

Opposing Viewpoints: Community Policing presents the debate over community policing in the following chapters: "How Should Community Policing Be Implemented?," "Are Community Policing and Neighborhood Watch Programs Effective?," "How Can Community Policing Be Improved?," and "Do Stand Your Ground Laws Empower Citizens?" The contrasting perspectives and analyses collected in this volume represent the challenges of maintaining law and order at the neighborhood level.

Notes

1. US Department of Justice, "FY 2014 Performance Budget," March 29, 2013. www.justice.gov/jmd/2014justification/pdf/cops-justification.pdf.
2. US Department of Justice, "FY 2014 Performance Budget."
3. US Department of Justice, "FY 2014 Performance Budget."
4. *Journal of Public Economics*, "COPS and Crime," February 2007.
5. Quoted in Heritage Foundation, "Why Would COPS 2.0 Succeed When COPS 1.0 Failed?" *WebMemo* #1903, April 28, 2008. www.heritage.org/research/reports/2008/04/why-would-cops-20-succeed-when-cops-10-failed.
6. *Criminology*, "COPS Grants and Crime Revisited," February 2007.

OPPOSING
VIEWPOINTS®
SERIES

CHAPTER 1

How Should Community Policing Be Implemented?

Chapter Preface

In problem-oriented policing (POP), the root causes of crime and disorder are identified and assessed to create law-enforcement strategies, going beyond the "call-and-response" of traditional policing. Herman Goldstein, professor emeritus at the University of Wisconsin Law School, conceptualized POP in his well-known 1979 article "Improving Policing: A Problem-Oriented Approach." Goldstein argued that police agencies "have been particularly susceptible to the 'means over ends' syndrome, placing more emphasis in their improvement efforts on organization and operating methods than on the substantive outcome of their work." He proposed that agencies develop systematic processes to investigate criminal and anti-social behavior. "It requires identifying these problems in more precise terms, researching each problem, documenting the nature of the current police response, assessing its adequacy and the adequacy of existing authority and resources, engaging in a broad exploration of alternatives to present responses, weighing the merits of these alternatives, and choosing from among them," Goldstein maintained.

In 1987, criminal justice experts John E. Eck and William Spelman expanded the POP approach with the four-stage SARA (Scanning, Analysis, Response, and Assessment) model. In the "scanning" stage, police identify chronic problems in the jurisdiction, aiming to detect patterns in crime. Next, in the "analysis" stage, information and data on offenders, victims, and crimes are analyzed in order to develop responses and interventions. Then, in the "response" stage, police develop and implement the responses and interventions in the jurisdiction. Finally, the effectiveness of police responses and interventions, as well as how they are executed, is measured in the "assessment" stage.

The Office of Community Oriented Policing Services (COPS), an agency of the US Department of Justice, has incorporated POP into its community-policing strategies, aiding in the creation of materials and tools for police agencies and funding the Center for Problem-Oriented Policing, stating that "POP offers police a multifaceted approach to solving problems and preventing new ones from occurring." The viewpoints in the following chapter present varying opinions on what community policing is, its strategies and goals, and how it differs from traditional policing.

"*Community Policing . . . not only addresses community concerns, but it is a philosophy . . . [of] empowering the community rather than dictating to the community.*"

Community Policing Solves Problems in Partnership with the Community

Victor E. Kappeler and Larry K. Gaines

Victor E. Kappeler is associate dean and foundation professor at the School of Justice Studies at Eastern Kentucky University. Larry K. Gaines is professor and chair of the Criminal Justice Department at Sam Houston State University in Texas. In the following viewpoint, the authors explain the concepts of community policing. It expands the police's mission from crime and law enforcement to engagement with the community to create solutions to neighborhood issues and quality of life, contend Kappeler and Gaines. Along with enforcing the law, the authors maintain, police officials also advise, facilitate, support, and lead community-based initiatives as well as encourage grassroots participation. Nonetheless, Kappeler and Gaines assert, community policing remains misunderstood despite its successes.

Victor E. Kappeler and Larry K. Gaines, "Chapter 1: The Idea of Community Policing," from *Community Policing: A Contemporary Perspective*, Anderson Publishing, 2011. Copyright © 2011 by Anderson Publishing. All rights reserved. Reproduced by permission.

As you read, consider the following questions:

1. How do the authors describe the two primary components of community policing?

2. What are the responsibilities of community policing officers (CPOs) in facilitating positive change, as stated by the authors?

3. How is community policing different from problem-oriented policing and community-oriented policing, according to Kappeler and Gaines?

Community policing is the first substantive reform in the American police institution since it embraced the professional model nearly a century ago. It is a dramatic change in the philosophy that determines the way police agencies engage the public. It incorporates a philosophy that broadens the police mission from a narrow focus on crime and law enforcement to a mandate encouraging the exploration of creative solutions for a host of community concerns—including crime, fear of crime, perceptions of disorder, quality of life, and neighborhood conditions. Community policing, in its ideal form, not only addresses community concerns, but it is a philosophy that turns traditional policing on its head by empowering the community rather than dictating to the community. In this sense, policing derives it role and agenda from the community rather than dictating to the community. Community policing rests on the belief that only by working together with people will the police be able to improve quality of life. This implies that the police must assume new roles and go about their business in a very different way. In addition to being law enforcers, they must also serve as advisors, facilitators, supporters, and leaders of new community-based initiatives. The police must begin to see themselves as part of the community rather than separate from the community. In its ideal form, community policing is a grassroots form of participa-

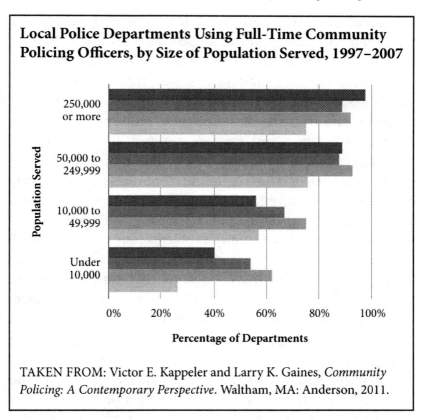

Local Police Departments Using Full-Time Community Policing Officers, by Size of Population Served, 1997–2007

TAKEN FROM: Victor E. Kappeler and Larry K. Gaines, *Community Policing: A Contemporary Perspective*. Waltham, MA: Anderson, 2011.

tion, rather than a representative top-down approach to addressing contemporary community life. In this sense, police become active participants in a process that changes power configurations in communities. It empowers the police to bring real-life problems of communities to those governmental authorities with the capacity to develop meaningful public policy and provide needed services to their communities.

Two Primary Components

Community policing consists of two primary components: community partnerships and problem solving. It is a partnership or enhanced relationship between the police and the community they serve. It is a partnership in that the police must assist people with a multitude of problems and social conditions including crime, and it is a partnership because the police must solicit support and active participation in dealing with these problems. It is an enhanced relationship, since the police must deal with substantive issues. They must go beyond merely responding to crime and calls for service. They must recognize and treat the causes of these problems so that they are resolved. When problems are resolved, there is a higher level of civility and tranquility in a community. Thus, the two primary components of community policing are community partnerships and problem solving. Community partnerships are the engagement by the police with the community to co-operatively resolve community problems. On the other hand, problem solving is where community policing officers (CPOs) attempt to deal with the conditions that cause crime and negatively affect the quality of life in a community. Problem solving is an important part of community policing.

Community policing also embodies an organizational strategy that allows police departments to decentralize service and reorient patrol. The focus is on the police officer who works closely with people and their problems. This CPO has responsibility for a specific beat or geographical area, and works as a generalist who considers making arrests as only one of many viable tools, if only temporarily, to address community problems. As the community's conduit for positive change, the CPO enlists people in the process of policing and improving the quality of life in a community. The CPO serves as the community's ombudsman to other public and private agencies that can offer help. If police officers are given stable assignments to geographical areas, they are able not only to focus on current problems, but also to become directly involved in strategies that may forestall long-range problems. Also, by giving people the power to set local police agendas, community policing challenges both police officers and community members to cooperate in finding new and creative ways to accurately identify and solve problems in their communities.

What started as an experiment using foot patrols and problem solving in a few departments exploded into a national mandate. As a result of the Violent Crime Control and Law Enforcement Act of 1994 and its provision to fund 100,000 more CPOs, most police departments in the United States now say they [sub]scribe to community policing. In the 1990s, community policing became an institutionalized and publicly understood form of policing. In 2010, [law-enforcement researcher Brian A.] Reaves reported that 53 percent of police departments have community policing as part of their mission statements. . . .

Community policing has become an important part of policing in all but the smallest police departments.

Even the media presented a limited but very positive depiction of community policing. "Community policing, or variations of it, has become the national mantra of American policing. Throughout the United States, the language, symbolism, and programs of community policing have sprung up in urban, suburban, and even rural police departments". Additionally, community policing became a standard in many other countries. Police departments all over the world embraced the language of community policing. It has become ingrained throughout departments as managers attempt to develop strategies and tactics to deal with day-to-day issues and community problems.

Substantial Confusion

Despite this impressive progress, many people, both inside and outside police departments, do not know precisely what "community policing" is and what it can do. Although most everyone has heard of community policing, and most police departments say that they have adopted the philosophy, few actually understand how it works and the possibilities it has for police agencies and communities. Indeed, it is viewed from a number of different perspectives. Is community policing simply a new name for police-community relations? Is it foot patrol? Is it crime prevention? Is it problem solving? Is it a political gimmick, a fad, or a promising trend, or is it a successful new way of policing? Perhaps [criminal justice specialist] David Bayley best summarized the confusion about community policing:

> Despite the benefits claimed for community policing, programmatic implementation of it has been very uneven. Although widely, almost universally, said to be important, it means different things to different people—public relations campaigns, shop fronts, and mini-stations, re-scaled patrol beats, liaisons with ethnic groups, permission for rank-and-file to speak to the press, Neighborhood Watch, foot patrols, patrol-detective teams, and door-to-door visits by police officers. Community policing on the ground often seems less a program than a set of aspirations wrapped in a slogan.

There is substantial confusion surrounding community policing. It stems from a variety of factors that, if not attended to, can undermine a department's efforts to successfully implement community policing. The sources of confusion are:

- Community policing's introduction into American policing has been a long, complicated process. It is rooted in team policing, police-community relations, and crime prevention;

- Some police departments are using community policing as a cover for aggressive law enforcement tactics rather than serving the needs of their communities. When this happens, confusion arises about a police department's real commitment to the community;

- The movement continues to suffer because some police departments claim to have implemented community policing, but they violate the spirit or the letter of what true community policing involves and demands;

• Most police agencies have adopted the language of community policing, but have yet to change their organizational structures and value systems to bring them into line with the community policing philosophy;

• Community policing threatens the status quo, which always generates resistance and spawns controversy within police organizations. This is because community policing challenges basic beliefs, which have become the foundation for traditional policing. It requires substantive changes in the way police officers and commanders think, the organizational structure of police departments, and the very definition of police work;

• Community policing may generate public expectations that go unfulfilled, thus creating a backlash against community policing and the department;

• Community policing is often confused with problem-oriented policing and community-oriented policing. Community policing is not merely problem-oriented policing or becoming "oriented" toward the community. While community policing does use problem-solving approaches, unlike problem-oriented policing community policing always engages the community in the identification of and solution to problems rather than seeing the police as the sole authority in this process.

"*Traditional policing activities . . . are not at odds with community policing; rather, community policing calls for a slightly different perspective.*"

Community Policing Is Different from Traditional Policing

Matthew Scheider

In the following viewpoint, Matthew Scheider asserts that traditional policing responds after the occurrence of crime, but community policing is more strategic and considered in its approach. For example, Scheider says that unlike traditional policing, community policing views arrests as one of many responses in the long-term solution of crime, including reducing access to potential victims and changing the features of neighborhoods that generate criminal activity. Additionally, in community policing, the flow of law enforcement information is broadened among agencies and other entities in the community, including businesses, individuals, and the media. Matthew Scheider is assistant director of the Office of Community Oriented Policing Services (COPS), an arm of the US Department of Justice.

Matthew Scheider, "The Role of Traditional Policing in Community Policing," *Community Policing Dispatch*, vol. 1, no. 3, March 2008. Reproduced by permission.

As you read, consider the following questions:

1. How does routine patrol differ in community policing than in traditional policing, in Scheider's view?

2. What does community policing encourage in rapid response to calls for service, as explained by the author?

3. In Scheider's view, what do investigations call for in community policing?

Traditionally, police organizations have responded to crime after it occurs and, therefore, are structured to support routine patrol, rapid response to calls for service, arrests, and follow-up investigation. Community policing calls for a more strategic and thoughtful incorporation of these aspects of police business into an overall broader police mission focused on the proactive prevention of crime and disorder.

Routine Patrol

Community policing advocates for the strategic application of routine patrol that is conducted with an eye toward desired outcomes. Rather than just conducting routine patrol because "that is how we have always done it," routine patrol should be part of comprehensive problem-reduction and community outreach strategies. Routine patrol, for example, may be used specifically to increase police visibility to reduce fear of crime; or preventive patrol may be increased in a particular hot-spot neighborhood as part of a larger comprehensive crime-reduction strategy.

Rapid Response to Calls for Service

Community policing advocates for the strategic application of rapid response. For the vast majority of police calls for service, decreases in response times do not increase the chances of arrest or prevent harm to victims. Community policing encourages the police and the public to determine how rapid a response is necessary based on the nature of the call for service and to align expectations to match these policies. Community policing also encourages the police to increase the means by which citizens are able to report incidents, such as through online reporting systems or the use of trained volunteers who take police reports. These efforts should increase the time available to focus on the development of strategic responses to crime problems.

Arrests

It is well-known to police practitioners and police scholars that the police can seldom arrest their way out of crime and social-disorder problems. Although arrests will always be a vital and important function of the police, arrests alone generally are not an effective nor efficient way to develop long-term solutions to crime problems, particularly considering that the vast majority of offenses do not result in arrest. Community policing views arrests as one potential response among many available to the police. Part of the proposed solution to any serious public safety problem likely involves arresting offenders (particularly targeting high-volume repeat offenders). For police activity to bring about long-term solutions to crime and disorder problems, however, a wider variety of responses that limit criminal opportunities and access to victims and decrease the crime-generating features of particular geographic places are typically necessary.

Investigations

Conducting investigations (large and small) will always be central to the police mission. Community policing encourages agencies to have strong investigative functions in order to solve crimes, and also asks law enforcement to enhance the value of these investigations by linking them to broader problem-solving activities. Community policing calls both for full-time investigators and for individual officers who take in-

In Community Policing, All Officers Must Be Involved

If community policing is to become a department-wide commitment, all officers must become involved. All officers on patrol, not just community policing officers, must exit their scout cars and interact daily with the citizens. Officers must demonstrate this way of policing to new officers so it will be viewed as the "normal" way to patrol. The entire department should eventually be trained, and this can be achieved three ways. Firstly, academy training will train new recruits on this type of approach. Since these officers have not been conditioned any other way, this will be most effective. Secondly, field training shows officers already on patrol, how to become more effective as problem solvers. The third method of training is an ongoing in-service training which constantly updates and improves current practices.

Dwayne Love,
Community Policing: Building Relationships,
Detroit Police Department, 2002.

cident reports to gather and share information to inform crime-prevention efforts. Investigations of thefts from construction sites, for example, can be enhanced by including information about building completion, the names of builders, the status of surrounding buildings, or the security level of the site. Investigations of known gang members and gang affiliations can feed efforts to understand gang relationships that can be used to inform comprehensive gang-reduction strategies. Information gathered through sound investigative techniques can serve as a vital resource to feed problem analysis efforts designed to develop lasting solutions to problems.

Law Enforcement Information Sharing

Finally, traditional policing has generally emphasized the role of partnerships and information sharing with other law enforcement entities at the state, local, and federal level. Information about known or suspected offenders is often shared. Community policing advocates for a broader flow of information between law enforcement agencies regarding potentially effective solutions to crime and disorder problems and crime trends and patterns. It also calls for police to broaden the array of potential partnerships beyond other law enforcement entities to include nonprofits, businesses, nonlaw enforcement government agencies, individual community members, and the media. Moreover, these partnerships should involve more than the sharing of crime or other relevant information with these groups, but rather should be focused on developing proactive long-term solutions to problems that are of concern to citizens.

A Slightly Different Perspective

Traditional policing activities are at the core of most police departments. These activities are not at odds with community policing; rather, community policing calls for a slightly different perspective. Slight modifications and changes in perspective regarding traditional policing activities can make a significant contribution toward advancing the community policing philosophy and thereby increase the capacity of police agencies to deliver fair, effective, and efficient police services.

> "Community policing is rooted in law enforcement's dependence on the public's eyes, ears, information and influence to exert social control."

Community Policing Requires the Involvement and Understanding of Communities

Linda S. Miller, Kären Matison Hess, and Christine Hess Orthmann

In the following viewpoint, Linda S. Miller, Kären Matison Hess, and Christine Hess Orthmann describe the ways in which citizens are involved in community policing efforts. First, however, the authors emphasize that it is not considered community policing itself. As explained by the authors, citizen involvement in law enforcement includes overseeing police performance through civilian review boards, forming citizen patrol groups, attending police academy programs for nonofficers, and volunteering at police departments. The authors suggest that each program has potential advantages and drawbacks. Miller is a retired sergeant with the Bloomington, Minnesota, police department and is the

Linda S. Miller, Kären M. Hess, and Christine Hess Orthman, *Community Policing: Partnerships for Problem Solving.* Delmar Cengage, 2011, pp. 78–84. © 2011 Cengage Learning.

former executive director of the Upper Midwest Community Policing Institute. The late Kärin Matison Hess was an instructor at Normandale Community College in Bloomington, Minnesota. Christine Hess Orthmann is the owner of Orthmann Writing & Research, Inc.

As you read, consider the following questions:

1. Why do police often maintain that civilian review boards are unfair, as stated by the authors?

2. How did the Fairlawn Coalition, a citizen patrol, drive drug dealers away from their area, as told by Miller, Hess, and Orthmann?

3. In the authors' view, what benefits can citizen volunteers provide to the community?

Once upon a time, when food resources in a village were seemingly gone, a creative individual—knowing that each person always has a little something in reserve—proposed that the community make stone soup.

After a stone was set to boil, people in the community were asked if they had "just a little something" to improve the soup. One person found a carrot, another brought a few potatoes, another brought a bit of meat and so on. When the soup was finished, it was thick and nourishing. Such is the situation in our communities today. Because resources are stretched to the limit, people tend to hold on to their time, talent or money. These self-protective actions leave most groups without enough resources to effectively handle community problems. Perhaps it is time to adopt the "stone soup" stance of cooperation.

Community members have a high interest level in their local police departments and have been involved in a variety of ways for many years. This involvement, although it establishes important contact, should not be mistaken for community policing. It usually does not involve the partnerships and problem-solving activities of community policing.

Civilian Review Boards

The movement for citizen review has been a major political struggle for more than 40 years and remains one of the most controversial issues in police work today. According to the New York City Civilian Complaint Review Board (CCRB) there are approximately 90 civilian oversight agencies around the country. These agencies take different forms and frequently have different jurisdictions and powers. The CCRB is the largest civilian oversight agency in the United States and investigates complaints of excessive or unnecessary use of force, abuse of authority, discourtesy and offensive language. The CCRB refers complaints about corruption or neglect of duty to the police department.

Supporters of civilian review boards believe it is impossible for the police to objectively review actions of their colleagues and emphasize that the police culture demands that police officers support each other, even if they know something illegal has occurred. Opponents of civilian review boards stress that civilians cannot possibly understand the complexities of the policing profession and that it is demeaning to be reviewed by an external source.

Currently, most departments handle officer discipline internally, with department personnel investigating complaints against officers and determining whether misconduct occurred.

In Favor of Civilian Oversight

Citizens who demand to be involved in the review process maintain that internal police discipline is tantamount to allowing the "fox to investigate thefts in the chicken coop." According to these citizens, police protect each other and cover up improper or illegal conduct. Citizens believe that this perpetuates abuses and sends a message to brutal officers that their behavior will be shielded from public scrutiny.

In some larger cities, police have lost the power to investigate complaints against fellow officers. The trend is toward more openness and citizen involvement in these matters. Officers should assume they will be required to be more accountable for their actions. Officers may be held to a higher standard and will need to be prepared to justify their use of force in certain situations.

In Opposition to Civilian Oversight

Theoretically, citizen review boards offer an efficient and effective means of identifying officer misdeeds and reconciling them to the satisfaction of the community at large. However, although civilian review boards may be good in theory, they are often poor in reality. They frequently fail to operate objectively, lack impartial or specialized agents to conduct essential investigations and are devoid of any enforcement power needed to carry out their recommendations. Furthermore, the people who volunteer to serve on a board are not necessarily representative of the community and, in many cases, are "vocal rabble rousers" who wish to impose their values on the community. Opponents to civilian review boards cite such shortcomings as reasons to do without these ineffectual entities.

Police often maintain it would be unfair to allow those outside police work to judge their actions because only police officers understand the complexities of their job and, in particular, how and when they must use force. They stress that few citizens understand such concepts as "command presence" and "verbal force" so often necessary in high-risk encounters. As one police sergeant put it: "The public should walk a mile in our combat boots before they judge us."

Opponents also argue that police should have full responsibility for managing their own conduct just as other professionals such as physicians and lawyers do.

Striking a Balance

Successful resolution of this issue requires that the concerns of both the community and the police be addressed. The desired outcome would be that the police maintain the ability to perform their duties without the fear that they will be second-guessed, disciplined or sued by those who do not understand the difficulties of their job. Successful oversight agencies do not simply investigate complaints; they proactively seek the underlying causes of police misconduct or problems.

Citizen Patrol

Community policing is rooted in law enforcement's dependence on the public's eyes, ears, information and influence to exert social control. In some communities citizens' attempts to be those eyes and ears have emerged in the form of citizen patrols. Some citizen patrols have formed as part of partnerships with the local police department, some independent of police partnerships and some in the face of police opposition. It is difficult for citizen volunteers, especially those in citizen patrols formed in spite of police opposition, to win the respect, trust and support of the police, who often have strong opinions about civilian involvement in what they consider police business or see citizens as critics of department efforts.

The Alliance of Guardian Angels, an organization that bills itself as serving communities, is controversial. Headed by a high-profile figure, Curtis Sliwa, and his wife, they go to communities having street crime problems and offer to patrol the streets and make citizen arrests. The members all wear red berets and are usually unarmed. Typically, citizens approve of the Guardian Angels, who they think are making their community safe. Local police, however, are not usually happy to have the Guardian Angels in their communities, often viewing them as untrained vigilantes who do not know the community, often provoke incidents and sometimes use physical force. For example, in Boston, the police commissioner "spurned" their offer to bring their red berets and street patrols, calling them unwelcome. In February 2009, the mayor of Norwalk, Connecticut, was "unhappy" with a confrontation between a group of youths and the Guardian Angels, repeating his stance that the crime-fighting group had no role in the city.

Citizen patrols are not new. The sheriffs' posses that handled law enforcement in America's Wild West have evolved to present-day citizen patrols, reserve police programs and neighborhood-watch groups. Many of the citizen patrols established throughout the country focus on the drug problem. For example, the Fairlawn Coalition in Washington, DC, established nightly patrol groups to walk the streets of Fairlawn and act as a deterrent to drug trafficking. Wearing bright orange hats, the citizen patrols drove drug dealers from their positions simply by standing out on the streets with them and later by bringing in video cameras, still cameras and much publicity. The citizen group decided not to invite the Guardian Angels or Nation of Islam to help them, fearing their aggressive tactics could escalate into violence. They chose instead to include men and women aged 40 and older to create a presence on the street but to pose no threat to the physical well-being of dealers.

The Blockos in Manhattan, New York, used a similar approach. To combat street-level drug dealing in their middle-class neighborhood, residents held some meetings and decided to go out into the street as a group and stand near the dealers. They also had a graphic artist provide posters to announce their meetings, and a member persuaded the *New York Times* to publish a story on their efforts.

Another tactic was used in Manhattan by a group called 210 Stanton, referring to the address of a building that was headquarters of a major drug-selling operation. Community patrol officers guarded the entrances to the building, requiring all visitors to sign in. If the visitors were going to the apartment where the drug dealing was occurring, officers accompanied them. In addition, information provided by residents helped solidify the case against the resident of the apartment where most of the drug dealing was taking place. Search warrants were issued, charges filed and the resident convicted.

In Arizona, ranchers near the Mexican border have formed the American Border Patrol (ABP), a citizens' patrol group whose goal is to help the official U.S. Border Patrol by finding and detaining illegal immigrants crossing into America from Mexico. They claim to have apprehended and turned over about 10,000 illegal immigrants to the Border Patrol in the past 5 years. Federal law enforcement agencies are not enthusiastic about the patrols. The U.S. Border Patrol does not comment on the matter but clearly is against any citizen activities beyond observing illegal activity and calling them for help.

Some citizen groups have exchange programs to reduce the chance of retribution by local drug dealers. Such exchange programs provide nearby neighborhoods with additional patrols while reducing the danger. Local dealers are less likely to recognize a vigil-keeper who lives in another neighborhood.

Citizen Police Academies

Another type of community involvement is through citizens' police academies (CPAs) designed to familiarize citizens with law enforcement and to keep the department in touch with the community. Police academies, which are popular with police departments and citizens, have the benefit of building community support for law enforcement and of helping citizens understand the police. . . .

In 1985 Orlando, Florida, hosted its first CPA and reports that it was an immediate success. Since that time more than

The Police Do Not Have a Monopoly on Security

It is equally important for the government, the police, and the justice system to recognize that they do not have a monopoly on creating and maintaining security. A strong criminal justice system and a visible police presence are important in shaping social order, but they should not be depended upon exclusively. A free society can be threatened by an over-reliance on tough enforcement, punishment, and prison as the primary means for establishing order and safety. The key lies in balancing the formal system of control with informal means of regulation so there can be a coproduction of public safety.

Caroline G. Nicholl,
Community Policing, Community Justice,
and Restorative Justice, *1999.*

1,000 community-oriented citizens have graduated from the program. The program is free of charge and offered twice a year. The class lasts for 12 to 14 weeks and is held for 3 hours in the evening. Topics include uniformed patrol, special operations, criminal investigation and youth/criminal law. The CPA also offers elective field trips to the jail and a ride-along with a uniformed patrol officer. In 2000 the department hosted its first CPA for senior citizens, held at one of the senior centers during the day.

The Arlington (Texas) Police Department began a CPA for Spanish-speaking residents in 1999 and has since developed an 8-week Asian CPA designed to teach Asian residents how the department functions. Detectives explain how investigations are conducted for homicides, robberies, wrecks, juvenile crimes and gangs.

The Palm Beach (Florida) Police Department has a Teen Police Academy for students aged 13 to 16. The program includes classroom instruction, hands-on training and field trips. Many departments around the country have developed similar programs.

In addition to regular CPAs and CPAs for seniors, teens and specific ethnic groups, some departments have developed alumni CPAs. Any of these endeavors can result in a large pool of willing volunteers for police department projects.

Research by [clinical psychologist JoAnne] Brewster and colleagues found that a CPA can improve the image of the police and increase the public's willingness to cooperate: "Overall, opinions about CPAs are favorable, and studies show that citizen participants and police personnel gain a number of benefits." A survey of 92 graduates from one CPA found that citizens were more educated about law enforcement, more realistic in their evaluation of media accounts and more willing to volunteer for police projects.

Citizen Volunteers

Volunteers supplement and enhance existing or envisioned functions, allowing law enforcement professionals to do their jobs more effectively. They can provide numerous benefits to a department, including maximizing existing resources, enhancing public safety and services and improving community relations. Other services that volunteers may provide include fingerprinting children, patrolling shopping centers, checking on homebound residents and checking the security of vacationing residents' homes. Clerical and data support, special event planning, search and rescue assistance, grant writing and transporting mail between substations also can be done by volunteers. Volunteers in Public Service (VIPS) is one of five Citizen Corps partner programs. The International Association of Chiefs of Police (IACP) manages and implements the VIPS program in partnership with, and on behalf of, the White

House Office of the USA Freedom Corps and the Bureau of Justice Assistance, Office of Justice Programs, U.S. Department of Justice. The VIPS program provides support and resources for agencies interested in developing or enhancing a volunteer program and for citizens who wish to volunteer their time and skills with a community law enforcement agency. The program's ultimate goal is to enhance the capacity of state and local law enforcement to utilize volunteers. Through this program, the VIPS staff seeks to

- Learn about promising practices being used in existing VIPS programs and share this information with law enforcement agencies that want to expand their programs,

- Increase the use of volunteers in existing programs,

- Help citizens learn about and become involved in VIPS programs in their communities, and

- Help agencies without volunteer programs get them started (VIPS Web site, 2009).

Use of volunteers is increasing in law enforcement departments across the country. The Bellevue (Washington) Police Department usually has about 60 volunteers who contribute approximately 11,000 hours annually, saving the department roughly $187,000 a year. Using volunteers does more than just save money—it adds value to department services and enhances community policing efforts.

[Senior program manager at the International Association of Chiefs of Police Nancy] Kolb cautions that establishing and maintaining a volunteer program is not cost free but that the return on the investment is substantial. For example, the San Diego Police Department, in 2004, reportedly spent about $585,000 on the staffing, equipment and management of its four volunteer programs but estimates the value of the hours contributed by volunteers at more than $2.65 million. In another example, the Billings (Montana) Police Department was helped by volunteers doing computer work at what it estimated to be a billable value of $30,000.

It is important to note that citizen involvement in understanding and helping to police their communities is very important, but it, in itself, is *not* community policing. At the heart of the community policing philosophy is an emphasis on partnerships and on problem solving.

"*[Citzen policing attempts] are most powerful . . . when they are backed up by the implicit threat of calling the police.*"

Community Policing Without the Police? The Limits of Order Maintenance by the Community

David Thacher

In the following viewpoint, David Thacher contends that law enforcement through community policing requires police participation. First, he points out that advocates of community policing do not have clear alternatives to maintaining the peace. And while it is proposed that citizens can act to prevent crime and disorder, only the police, Thacher argues, can legitimately use physical force and restrain offenders. Moreover, forms of community-based crime prevention are most effective when they are supported by the police, he adds. Thacher is an associate professor of public policy and urban planning at the University of Michigan.

David Thacher, "Chapter 4: Community Policing Without the Police? The Limits of Order Maintenance by the Community," *Community Policing and Peacekeeping*, edited by Peter Grabosky, Reproduced with permission of Taylor and Francis in the format Republish in a book via Copyright Clearance Center.

As you read, consider the following questions:

1. What would occur without efforts to regulate disorder, as alleged by the author?

2. In Thacher's opinion, what is the real debate about order maintenance?

3. Why are the least formal social sanctions not an effective tool in order maintenance, in the author's view?

The proper role for the police in combating disorder has sparked controversy for as long as the police have existed. Recently much of this debate has been about whether "public order" is a worthwhile goal at all, but the debate also raises a different question: If we want our public spaces to be orderly, who should have the responsibility for maintaining that order? In principle, the police are not the only possible answer to this question, since a variety of other community institutions might take responsibility for order maintenance. It is in that context that I mean to examine the wisdom of community policing without the police.

This question may appear unimportant simply because much of the recent criminological literature has been skeptical about the importance of public order. If order is not an important goal, there is no point in asking who should have responsibility for it. In the end, however, this skeptical position is untenable. Disorderly behavior such as verbal harassment of women, obstruction of busy thoroughfares, noise pollution, flagrant public urination, and deliberate intimidation make unfair use of public spaces. Even if it turned out that these actions do not contribute to a feeling of lawlessness that emboldens more serious criminals, they are still wrong, and our public spaces would be better off without them. Without any attempt to regulate disorder, the very existence of shared public spaces becomes precarious, as city dwellers disengage from the world around them and retreat into segregated environments where they will not encounter conflict in the first place.

Despite appearances to the contrary, even the most radical critics of police order maintenance concede that disorder should be regulated. Richard Sennett's *Uses of Disorder*, for example, is not really a defense of disorder. It is an argument that neighborhood residents rather than government officials ought to regulate it. Sennett worried that modern society insulates us too well from the need to deal with conflict, so that personality development remains stuck in a self-centered adolescence in which we ignore the concrete demands made by other people. As treatment for this modern personality disease, Sennett did prescribe more exposure to a "challenging social matrix," and this is the sense in which he "wants more disorder". Simply experiencing disorder, however, was not enough for Sennett; he believed that true personality development requires actual engagement with conflict through attempts to resolve it. Thus, what was needed was "not simply . . . places where the inhabitants encountered dissimilar people; the critical need is for men to have to deal with the dissimilarities". To accomplish that goal, Sennett believed that state regulatory bodies (including police but also other agencies, like land use authorities) should step aside to allow neighborhood residents to cope with conflicts themselves:

> If the kids were playing records loudly, late at night, no cop would come to make them turn the record player off—the police would no longer see to that kind of thing. If a bar down the street were too noisy for the children of the neighborhood to sleep, the parents would have to squeeze the bar owner themselves, by picketing or informal pressure, for no zoning laws would apply throughout the city.

Sennett sought to ensure that "men and women must deal with each other as people" in order to block "the flight into abstraction" that allows personality development to stall in adolescence.

Less elaborate considerations have led other critics to support some form of community-based order maintenance. In keeping with his "left realist" emphasis on the importance of public safety to the urban poor, Roger Matthews acknowledges that public order is important, but he insists that the ambiguity surrounding the proper meaning of disorder makes it unwise for police to play a role in regulating it, since the task will draw them into conflicts among different community factions and thereby risk "alienating sections of the community". More simply, police order maintenance is like swatting flies with heavy armor: Mobilizing a "heavy handed, truncheon-wielding army of police officers" to regulate disorder is simply an overreaction. In place of the heavy hand of the police, Matthews advocates a larger role for community institutions in order maintenance, pointing to recent disorder reduction initiatives where police played a subordinate role or no role at all.

Community as Police

It is not always clear what alternative to police order maintenance these critics have in mind. Sennett apparently envisions an anarchistic form of self-help—a world in which neighbors resolve their own disputes (in unspecified ways) rather than invoking the police or land use authorities. Urbanologist William Whyte similarly advocates self-policing by the users of public space, who may, for example, admonish a pedestrian who throws trash on the ground. Others advocate for more formal interventions. Matthews, for example, points to a recent resurgence of "various 'intermediary' agencies in regulating social (mis)behaviour," including "park-keepers, station guards . . . working mens' clubs, trade union associations, church organizations"; he goes on to mention unemployed adults enlisted as "transport officers" in a Dutch transit system and "concierges or receptionists" in British council estates. Bernard Harcourt similarly highlights the role that social workers, transit workers, and even publicly hired mimes can play in combating disorderly conduct, and Whyte emphasizes the importance of the informal "mayors" who occupy many public spaces—people like newsstand operators, building guards, and food vendors who have a long-term presence in a space that gives them the contextual knowledge and sense of ownership that order maintenance requires. Grabosky mentions civilian "wardens" in New Zealand who respond to public drunkenness and other forms of disorderly conduct (though he does not necessarily advocate this model).

The advocates for these alternative forms of order maintenance often emphasize the role these actors can play in preventing disorder, rather than their role in responding to it once it has it occurred. In general these proposals are uncontroversial: If it is possible to prevent subway fare beating through better turnstile design, few would oppose that strategy; indeed, leading advocates for a robust police role in order maintenance have endorsed it. But the question remains: What should be done when unacceptable disorder occurs despite society's best efforts to prevent it? Should the police play a role in regulating it? Should the task be left to other community institutions, or to no one at all? The real debate about the responsibility for order maintenance is primarily a debate about who, if anyone, should respond to various kinds of disorder when they actually occur—as they inevitably will, despite the vigorous preventative efforts that almost everyone endorses.

Disorder and the Function of the Police

The question of who should respond to disorder cannot be separated from the question of what types of response would be legitimate. Outright physical coercion is almost entirely the province of the police. If a man continually accosts passing women with epithets like "You're just a piece of meat to me, bitch" and refuses to stop when passers-by or Whyte's informal mayors scold him, the passers-by and the mayors have no legal authority to force him to stop. If anyone does, it is presumably the police, who largely monopolize the legitimate use of coercive force in our society. If we conclude that it is legitimate to physically restrain a man who behaves in this way after he defies less authoritative interventions, then the police are the only institutional vehicle available.

The question of whether the police ought to play a role in regulating disorder, then, is equivalent to the question of whether there are any types of disorder that fall into the category of things that it would be legitimate to put a stop to by resorting to coercive authority after other interventions have failed. To conclude that there are does not imply that police should always arrest the disorderly. It simply means that if less authoritative intervention fails, coercive action would be justified. The police are society's "or else", and if there is any form of disorder that justifies such a threat, then it is properly the business of police.

Managing Disorder

Police and community members alike may try to regulate disorder without forcibly restraining the perpetrators—for example, by cajoling or shaming the disorderly (Harcourt's publicly hired mimes who mock jaywalkers are one illustration) or by trying to persuade them to desist (Whyte's mayors typically seem to rely on this sort of remonstration). Again, community members ultimately have no legitimate recourse other than these informal interventions. Despite their arrest powers, however, even police often do not use them to maintain order.

The noncoercive interventions that police and community members alike use to maintain order can take many forms. At the informal extreme, Erving Goffman has described the social sanctions that all of us apply in everyday life to people who violate norms of public decorum (such as the ironic sanction of staring down someone who rudely stares). In

49

practice, however, these least formal social sanctions are not really viable tools for order maintenance because much of the disorderly behavior at the center of recent debates about public order would not occur in the first place if the person who engaged in it were sensitive to normal social pressure. (Goffman mentions "the drunk and the costumed" as illustrations of the idea that insulation from social pressure facilitates disorderly conduct.) If disorder arises precisely when the ordinary sanctions that underwrite everyday social interactions have broken down, some other means of controlling it will be necessary.

One possibility is the more deliberate efforts to exert social pressure that authors like Matthews, Whyte, and Harcourt have emphasized—the sustained and overt reprimands of disorderly conduct by food vendors, shopkeepers, security guards, and even mimes. These interventions are not authoritative in the way that police interventions are: If the person harassing women, blocking pedestrians, or flagrantly urinating refuses to stop, the vendor or shopkeeper cannot force him to. All the same, the forms of social pressure available to people other than the police can certainly be powerful.

They are most powerful, however, when they are backed up by the implicit threat of calling the police. During the 1970s and 1980s a large body of research examined the possibility of community-based crime prevention. A major conclusion of that literature was that informal social control works best when the threat of invoking formal authority backs it up. When that threat is perceived to be idle, informal control breaks down. It is precisely because the police would be authorized to take definitive coercive action (and because everyone involved knows they would) that many informal sanctions succeed. One study that reached this conclusion focused on the Priority Estates Project in Britain, which Matthews cites as a model of community-based order maintenance. One of ethnographer Janet Foster's interviewees in that research put the matter succinctly: "Community works in a lot of cases but obviously in some circumstances . . . [tenants] like to put the onus on the council or some legal authority". In this respect, community-based order maintenance is not an alternative to police order maintenance but a complement to it.

"Community policing and homeland security are not mutually exclusive policing philosophies."

Community Policing or Homeland Security: Sophie's Choice for Police?

Douglas Page

Based in Pine Mountain, California, Douglas Page is a writer and contributor to the law enforcement website Officer.com. In the following viewpoint, he writes that community policing and homeland security efforts, rather than undermining each other, do not conflict and in fact share commonalities. After the September 11, 2001, terrorist attacks, police departments shifted emphasis from community policing to counterterrorism efforts, damaging the relationship between authorities and communities, Page insists. Nonetheless, he says, the two overlap in how they approach and respond to crime and terrorism, especially when the latter is treated as crime. In fact, the author claims that community policing can help address civil rights issues in profiling terrorists and develop sources of intelligence within communities.

As you read, consider the following questions:

1. How do homeland security and community policing differ, as described by Page?

2. How did the September 11 attacks change how law enforcement agencies related to communities, according to the author?

3. What does Robert Friedmann, as cited by Page, state about realizing the role of local law enforcement in homeland security?

On Sept. 12, 2001, the Dearborn, Mich., Police Department put officers on 12-hour shifts for the first time in years. The purpose was so police could provide extra patrol around mosques, the Arab-American business district and schools with the largest Arab-American populations.

More than 200,000 (approximately 30 percent) of the Dearborn population was Arab-American at the time of the terror attacks. Police were concerned there might be retaliatory hate crimes, a well-founded fear. Hate crimes against Arabs and Muslims living in the United States increased by 1,700 percent in 2001, according to crime statistics compiled by the FBI.

"It didn't help when national media figures claimed there were 'celebrations' of the attacks in Dearborn by local Muslims, which was completely false," says David Thacher, a University of Michigan professor of public policy and urban planning. Thacher says a lot of the people who criticized the police about other things appreciated the extra protection that day. The Dearborn Police Department was later recognized in a Human Rights Watch report as the only local police department in the country that had responded appropriately at the time to the threat of hate crimes.

Thacher says the Dearborn PD example illustrates a larger point: that in terms of homeland security, local police should see its role as community protection—protecting its own community from the threat of terrorism, whether it's through preventative patrol against possible targets of attack, target hardening, investigating suspicious packages that arrive in the mail, or improving emergency response capabilities so they're prepared to minimize the damage if something happens.

On the other hand, when the local police get too involved in homeland security, which emphasizes surveillance, identification and investigation of particular people suspected of terrorism, this is often done at the expense of community policing, Thacher says. In policing, "homeland security" refers to police activities designed to prevent or respond to terrorism, whereas "community policing" emphasizes more traditional proactive policing, problem solving and community partnerships.

Toward the end of 2001, the Department of Justice initiated a voluntary interview project focused on about 5,000 Middle Eastern males holding temporary U.S. visas from countries where Al-Qaeda was known to have a strong terrorist presence. DOJ asked local police departments like the one in Dearborn to help do the interviews, hoping these males would voluntarily provide information that might be useful in the new war on terror.

"Not surprisingly, that move was a big source of tension between the Dearborn police and the Arab-American community," Thacher says. Many Arab-Americans believed the interviews were a form of ethnic profiling, and they feared heightened scrutiny from immigration officials. "Some people in the neighborhood found the interviews suspicious because they knew Dearborn police were working with federal agencies," Thacher says. "The community wondered if they were being spied on. They weren't, but local citizens weren't sure."

The federal request put Dearborn police in a difficult position. Officers were in general agreement with the federal plan, although most also understood and sympathized with the community. In response, Dearborn police organized working groups with Arab community leaders that were instrumental in changing several aspects of the DOJ plan, in order to reduce community concerns. In the end, Dearborn police agreed to help federal agents locate interviewees, and to accompany federal agents when the interviews were conducted. But local law enforcement officers declined to conduct any of the interviews themselves.

Thacher says terrorism investigation has to be predominantly a federal job because local police have a different job to do, namely focusing on community protection such as emergency response, target hardening, and preventative patrols, rather than terror surveillance and investigation.

In a 2005 paper in *Law & Society Review*, Thacher says the decentralized nature of the federal government places sharp limits on the ability of national policy makers to mobilize the great majority of the country's police officers to serve national goals. "If policy makers and the public conclude that these national goals have grown in importance relative to street crime, they may find it easier to shift resources toward federal police rather than reshape local policing."

Following the 9/11 attacks, many local police departments around the country expressed concerns about their ability to provide for homeland security without compromising traditional community policing responsibilities. Indeed, shortly after 9/11, several U.S. cities, Portland, Ore., among them, refused federal entreaties to interview young male immigrants from those countries believed to be harboring terrorists.

"Since community protection tasks lie squarely within the interests and competence of traditional police agencies, for most agencies the most promising and likely contribution of police to homeland security is likely to lie in this area," Thacher says. "The more dramatic and controversial area of offender search, by contrast, may fall more readily to national intelligence agencies like the FBI."

Terrorism Front Line

Most local police departments were put in the same difficult position as the Dearborn police following 9/11. The attacks changed just about everything in the United States, including how local law enforcement agencies relate to the communities they serve. Local police departments that had previously embraced community oriented policing policies to address crime suddenly found they were on the front lines in the war on terror. Some agencies changed their model of policing in order to embrace new homeland security responsibilities, a move encouraged by the federal government.

Washington recognized the enormous anti-terrorism resource local police potentially represented. There are more than 600,000 local police officers spread across nearly 13,000 autonomous local police departments in the United States, but there are only 12,000 FBI agents. Washington's shifting interests can be seen in funding swings. From 2001 to 2005, federal funding to the local police and first responder community increased from $616 million to $3.4 billion, most earmarked for homeland security.

The new emphasis on homeland security, however, often resulted in reduced community policing, which degraded community-police relationships, particularly in immigrant and Arab-American neighborhoods like Dearborn.

"After 9/11, community policing was shoved to the wayside as all budgets went to homeland security," says Robert Friedmann, a Georgia State emeritus professor of criminal justice and a member of the International Association of Chiefs of Police [IACP] Community Policing Committee. "Homeland security had immediate, clear, definable needs to protect people and property while community policing was, and still is, perceived more as a soft and complex approach."

Shortly after 9/11, IACP's Community Policing Committee formulated a resolution adopted by IACP general membership to promote community policing as an integral part of homeland security. "That resolution wasn't worth the paper it was written on because I doubt . . . serious thought was given to incorporating community policing as part of homeland security," Friedmann says.

That IACP committee provides annual awards to local police for excellence in community policing, with special mention given to those local police departments who try and combine the two. "The awards are few and far between," he says.

Friedmann says the problem began with the advent of community policing in the 1980s and 1990s, even before homeland security was an issue: "There was always more rhetoric than reality." Friedmann says community policing is not simply being more friendly with local citizens. Community policing means being proactive, developing partnerships, and addressing sources of crime as a precursor to reducing crime.

"The importance of this to homeland security is that the principles of being proactive and partnership-creation are extremely relevant to minimizing the likelihood of a terrorist incident. If someone in the community has information, you want them to provide that intelligence to you, but in order to do that you have to have developed good relationships in the community," he says.

Not "Sophie's Choice"

Law enforcement experts generally agree that community policing and homeland security are not mutually exclusive policing philosophies. It doesn't have to be a "Sophie's Choice," an impossible dilemma of either-or. The two missions actually share a number of commonalities. Friedmann says the informed local police chief needs to address both the threats of terrorism and provide responses to traditional crime. "The desired role of local law enforcement in homeland security policy is more fully realized when an agency employs community policing principles as an integral part of its homeland security efforts. Focusing only on counter-terrorism is no longer enough."

Friedmann says countries like Israel and England have found that focusing on terrorism will not suffice, since the public is more interested in traditional police services that address street crime and crimes against property. "You can't just simply say you're busy with terrorism," he says. "More people are affected by traditional crime than by terrorism."

The most apparent overlap between the two approaches relates to the manner in which they manage the prevention and response to crime and terrorism, particularly if terrorism is recognized as a criminal activity. Through this classification, the function of police departments coincides with the objectives of homeland security—the prevention, detection and eradication of criminal activity through effective law enforcement.

"When local police employ a community policing strategy, they not only satisfy the aims of domestic security, but also alleviate many of the known shortcomings that often plague these policies," Friedmann says.

Stanley Supinski, director of Partnership Programs at the Naval Postgraduate School's Center for Homeland Defense and Security, and an instructor in the Homeland Security Management Institute, Long Island University, says proven methodologies, especially those that serve to develop and improve ties to communities and constituents, can serve to support new law enforcement roles and missions—in this case homeland security.

"Research is clearly showing that implementing community oriented policing strategies and tactics can assist law enforcement agencies with preventing both crime and terrorism," Supinski writes in a recent Journal of Homeland Security and Emergency Management paper titled "Policing and Community Relations in the Homeland Security Era."

Supinski advocates a concept he calls "community oriented homeland security" that uses the concepts of community policing to not only support law enforcement, but also to engage the public, with a concept it understands, in all aspects of the homeland security enterprise.

"It goes beyond the prevention aspect to preparedness, response and recovery in the aftermath of disasters," he says. Supinski says the key is to develop and maintain strong, positive community relations that clearly support law enforcement's role in homeland security.

Achieving a balance between the two competing philosophies while preserving civil liberties at the same time can be a delicate matter, but other studies suggest that by adopting community policing principles it is possible to reduce civil rights violations associated with ethnic profiling performed behind the mask of homeland security. The idea is to develop a strong enough communication network between the police and public that false rumors so inaccurate reports of police operations can be prevented.

"Traditional intelligence methods have limited power to penetrate Middle Eastern communities," Supinski says. Instead, cooperation, along with solid communications networks and increased trust, allows police to develop sources for information inside the community, which could provide vital intelligence relating to potential terror activity.

"Otherwise, it will be impossible for intelligence officers to penetrate these communities," says Supinski.

> *"Community policing ... has a start date, which means it will have an end date."*

The Real Truth of Community Policing

William L. Harvey

William L. Harvey is the chief of police for the Ephrata Police Department in Pennsylvania and management contributor to Officer.com, a police website. In the following viewpoint, Harvey argues that community-policing programs are temporary, as they are dependent on disappearing federal funding. Community policing was once the "cash cow" for police departments, he states, but after the September 11, 2001, terrorist attacks, law enforcement monies have been redirected toward homeland security. Consequently, the programs died off, with very few agencies bankrolling their own, Harvey explains. Departments seeking to adopt community policing, he concludes, must now rely on private sources of support.

As you read, consider the following questions:

1. What does Harvey say about agencies that have community policing in their mission statement?

2. What is Harvey's advice for police chiefs who are pressured to adopt community policing?

3. According to the author, what was community policing to many agencies and politicians?

I recently read another city's newspaper headlines where their police chief was terminated by the incoming mayor. The rationale for the chief's dismissal was that the new mayor wanted a police chief that was fully committed to community policing. This city in question did not have a crime problem; that police chief was doing a good job according to the story writer; so, what was the real reason here? I would suspect the "P" word (politics), but I waited. When the job announcement for the new chief was released, the answer was in the first sentence: "a chief that is totally committed to community policing." I still did not believe; yet I was dangerously close to the truth. What is the real truth behind community policing today?

Going back to the reason for this article, I did not know this chief personally. Therefore, this is not some public defense. I did some deeper research. There was a change in political party affiliation with this new mayor. Those of us who have been in this business for several years know it all lies amongst political lines. During the Clinton administration, community policing was the catchword. It was the "cash cow" for every police agency and the city it served. Cities got money hand over fist. Equipment, personnel and overtime galore—this was a way to reach out and touch the masses. It was a good methodology to fill in some social gaps to the disadvantaged. Grants were the word of the day and it was community policing via any and every methodology known to mankind for a while. If you wanted foot, bike, or horse patrols, or substations—you got it! Then, when the new toy wasn't so shiny and cute anymore, some departments were called in to actually validate and bring in their grants within reason.

Now, it's post-9/11, and the Bush administration has had redirected most all law enforcement monies towards homeland security. All of the "feel good" programs have withered up and many have died because of a lack of local funding. The local tax dollar never supported the COPS programs; it was the federal money that was the deep pocket. It is difficult for a local chief or sheriff to get the troops to do these programs on their time; it was the grant money overtime that fueled the COPS train. This was especially prevalent in strongly unionized departments or those with strong contracts. To most, it was all about the money. However, there were some officers that were genuine about the mission. The truth is that is it is difficult to get jaded cops to sing "kum by ya" without money leading the choir.

What are the real truths here—the ones we must face but cannot say in a politically sensitive world? First and foremost, community policing was and will always be a program. Anytime you hear the word "program," take a clue. It has a start date, which means it will have an end date. Administrators, politicos, activists and chiefs must take heed here—programs will have a stopping point and they must prepare for the inevitable end. What will you do when the money train derails? Few did much preparation for this, except to cry foul. What department has fully accepted and bankrolled community policing without any federal, state or private funding? Answer: Not Many. They are few and far between. There are those who have the terms in their mission statement and use it in their rhetoric, but is it in a line item in their budget? Are they totally doing it on their taxpayer's backs? I know of none that are doing it. It was designed by the feds, and will always be on the federal dole. There were several departments I personally know of that jumped on the programs, but when the only money was through matching or descending grants, they started to distance themselves quietly. It is all about other people's money.

Community Policing Is Clearly Waning

In the current era, community policing is clearly waning. It had always suffered three problems. First, community policing, in its early form, was about policing minority communities in a way that involved the police working with minority citizens. It rapidly spread beyond that base, spurred in part by academic research carried out by researchers concerned about minorities in the U.S. Second, it was largely carried through federal programs that rewarded local agencies for particular programs. When the money ended so did the programs. Third, it never was effectively integrated into the line officer function. In many places where it was implemented, line personnel did not understand nor were effectively prepared for tasks that did not seem to have much to do with getting rough customers off the streets.

John P. Crank and Michael A. Cordero, Police Ethics: The Corruption of a Noble Cause *(Third Edition). Burlington, MA: Anderson Publishing, 2011.*

Secondly, for that chief who is about to be fired or those who have it written into their job contract—ask your employer to show you in federal or state codes where community policing is codified law. It is not a law, but rather a philosophy or mindset. This could possibly be a goal or project in your employee evaluation or performance contract.

I am not a total pessimist; community policing did some great things in bringing police and community together. It did open up lines of communication with our customer base. The problem is that we had that years ago and lost it. We must learn from history and not have to repeat this in another twenty years. Maintain what we have now, or in the not-too-distant future we will be reliving this all over again. History has a bad tendency to repeat itself, and this will be no different.

Finally, to many, this was a fill-in-the-gap for some social services that did not service the disadvantaged. To many politicians, this was rhetoric to be the great salve to the masses for votes. "If you vote for me; then the police will do this for you." As terrorism continues to be the top issue that moves emergency services and drains our resources, this will guide the grants and spending. As others clamor for community policing and free hot dogs and face painting, those days which may be gone, just like some chiefs and their federal grants. They will have to rely on private philanthropy and trusts to continue. To the new chief that takes that job: you had better get in good with the local grocery store for free sodas and goodies. You will need them for next block party. Your job will just may well depend on it.

Periodical and Internet Sources Bibliography

The following articles have been selected to supplement the diverse views presented in this chapter.

Mike Chalmers — "Some Cities Rethink How to Combat Crime," *USA Today*, October 18, 2011.

The Economist — "Cleaning Up the 'Hood; Policing Drug Sales," March 3, 2012.

Jason Vaughn Lee — "Policing After 9/11: Community Policing in an Age of Homeland Security," *Police Quarterly*, December 2010.

Tracey L. Meares — "The Good Cop: Knowing the Difference Between Lawful or Effective Policing and Rightful Policing—and Why It Matters," *William and Mary Law Review*, May 2013.

Ken Peak and Emmanuel P. Barthe — "Community Policing and CompStat: Merged, or Mutually Exclusive?," the *Police Chief*, December 2009.

Michael Powell — "Former Skeptic Now Embraces Divisive Tactic," *New York Times*, April 10, 2012.

Michael D. Reisig — "Community and Problem-Oriented Policing," *Crime & Justice*, July 2009.

Ann Richard — "Flint Community-Oriented Policing Seeks to Improve Public Safety," Charles Stewart Mott Foundation, May 26, 2011. www.mott.org.

Julie Spence — "Focusing on the Citizen: Julie Spence Discusses Some Fundamental Changes in the Way Policing Is Delivered to the Public," *Policing Today*, November 2008.

Kalee Thompson — "The Santa Cruz Experiment: Can a City's Crime Be Predicted and Prevented?," *Popular Science*, November 2011.

OPPOSING
VIEWPOINTS®
SERIES

CHAPTER 2

Are Community Policing and Neighborhood Watch Programs Effective?

Chapter Preface

In 1972, the National Sheriffs' Association established the National Neighborhood Watch Program in response to rising crime rates during the previous decade. It was funded by the US Department of Justice through its Law Enforcement Assistance Administration. "A Neighborhood Watch program is a group of people living in the same area who want to make their neighborhood safer by working together and in conjunction with local law enforcement to reduce crime and improve their quality of life," states the association, adding that "it is an opportunity to volunteer and work towards increasing the safety and security of our homes and our homeland." In its first two years, the program focused on increasing public awareness about robbery and "hard targeting," or securing a residence from breaking and entering, explains the Sheriffs' Association, then progressing to the watch groups of today.

Neighborhood Watch groups were formed under the direction of police agencies and called names like "crime watch" and "block watch." Activities may differ from group to group, including handing out information on preventing crime and patrolling neighborhoods, but are not limited to law enforcement. "Where disorder problems are the primary focus of Neighborhood Watch members, volunteers mobilize and conduct neighborhood cleanups, or work with faith-based organizations to assist with the homeless and mentally ill who wander the streets," says the Sheriffs' Association. Moreover, the association notes that these groups have grown from acting as the watchful "eyes and ears" of the community to promoting neighborhood pride and unity.

According to the 2000 National Crime Prevention Survey, 41 percent of Americans lived in communities and towns with Neighborhood Watch groups. "This makes Neighborhood

Watch the largest single organized crime-prevention activity in the nation," the survey claimed. In the following chapter, the authors debate the effectiveness of Neighborhood Watch programs, in addition to community-policing efforts, in the fight against crime.

> *"True community policing is what law enforcement was doing, without calling it that, 50 to 60 years ago."*

Community Policing Can Be Effective If Properly Practiced

Police Magazine

Police *is a publication for law enforcement officials. In the following viewpoint, it claims that community policing can be effective when patrol tactics and crime-fighting efforts make sense for the police department and its community. When properly practiced,* Police *contends, it emphasizes the individual initiatives and skills of officers as well as interacting with local citizens to build relationships. Additionally, the city or county's location and the number of available officers are other important factors to consider, it observes. A police department will find success with a community-policing program, the author suggests, when recognizing that it requires a different time frame than routine patrol work, and both approaches need support.*

As you read, consider the following questions:

1. How can the implementation of a community-policing program in a big city differ from that in a small town, in *Police's* view?

2. What are the activities of a Neighborhood Enforcement Team in Phoenix, Arizona, as described by the author?

3. According to *Police*, how did the Neighborhood Service Team in Boise, Idaho, successfully combat vandalism?

If there is a sacred cow grazing in the field of law enforcement, it can be named in two words: community policing. Mayors and town councils clamor for it. Police chiefs endorse it. However, many of these people have no real clear idea of what constitutes community policing and what benefit, if any, it might bring to their cities. Worse, they may not realize that the secret to the success of a community-policing program is the capabilities of patrol officers.

It's a good bet that if an agency hasn't formally instituted community-based policing programs, it has at least incorporated the lexicon into department operations. What were once known as patrol officers have become Neighborhood Contact Officers or Community Oriented Police Enforcement Officers, charged with the sometimes-fuzzy tasks of taking "ownership" of a problem, "coordinating resources," and "facilitating" its resolution.

All of this bureaucratic speak leaves many officers asking the key question: What ever happened to crime fighting?

Individual Initiative

Advocates of community policing say that crime fighting is incorporated into the goals of the community policing concept. They also say that when implemented properly, community policing emphasizes the individual initiative of patrol officers, not the strategies of bureaucrats.

"With community policing, the officer is the organizer," says Bruce Benson, a former deputy chief at the Flint (Mich.)

Police Department—the acknowledged birthplace of the U.S. community-oriented policing (COP) movement. "It's amazing what officers will do with their own skills and own time, if they have some control.

"Officers can see their accomplishments, and what they haven't accomplished, and can see new approaches," says Benson, who is now an associate professor at the Michigan State University School of Criminal Justice. "I don't know of any research that shows just patrol and response reduces crime . . . but if you do [community-policing style] problem solving, the cops have to solve the problem."

"Nobody on Patrol"

It's true that there is little or no research to show that traditional patrol policing reduces crime. Of course, what proponents of community policing often fail to mention is that pretty much the same can be said about community policing. It's hard to find other-than-anecdotal research that documents the ability of community-oriented policing to reduce crime rates over an extended time period.

In New York City, for example, COP-style efforts are credited with contributing to the city's well-publicized plummeting homicide rate, down from 2,245 murders in 1990 to 983 in 1996. But other factors were also at work, including an improving U.S. economy, declining prevalence of crack cocaine use, and a reduction in the size of the crime-prone adolescent-male population. There was also a surge in tax revenue that enabled the Big Apple to deploy some 5,000 new officers onto city streets between 1990 and 1994. No one reasonable is saying that there are no benefits associated with community-oriented police work. But COP may not be the be all and end all of law enforcement that it's been made out to be.

There's certainly nothing wrong with encouraging officers to leave the isolation of radio patrol cars, and interact with appreciative, law-abiding citizens, not just criminals. And just plain common sense tells us that when officers sponsor neighborhood meetings and walk their beats, the relationships that they build with the locals make it more likely that citizens will approach them and work with them when they are witnesses to or victims of a crime.

However, some departments make the mistake of enacting operational changes based on enthusiasm and theory, rather than the real-world opinions and experiences of rank-and-file officers themselves.

It's something that Ron DeLord, a former Dallas-area patrol officer and detective and current president of the Combined Law Enforcement Association of Texas (CLEAT), has seen happen repeatedly. Departments create attractive new and specialized assignments, without considering how personnel shifts will impact bread-and-butter patrol duties, or even how they fit in with seniority issues, civil service rules, or union contracts.

"Patrol is the forgotten division," DeLord says. "My premise [about community policing] is you have to start first by asking questions like: How does this impact patrol? Do I have enough people to do this? What do the officers think? And does it have an [actual] impact on crime? But in the United States, police chiefs just don't want to start finding out from the rank and file what the impact is going to be."

CLEAT, which represents almost 15,000 members and sponsors nearly 100 affiliated locals, is Texas' largest police union and is well positioned to monitor trends in the state. "When community policing started in Houston, it was called Neighborhood Oriented Policing (NOP), and the joke was that it stood for 'Nobody on Patrol'," he says. "[Management] pulled so many police officers off the street that the patrol division was overwhelmed with trying to keep up with the call load."

Country COP, City COP

How a community-oriented policing program is implemented often depends upon the location of the agency involved and the number of cops it can field. Big cities are generally strapped for budget and for officer labor, which means their community policing programs are sometimes an afterthought. In contrast, some departments, particularly those in towns and smaller cities, advocate infusing community-policing practices into all police-public interactions.

At one department, for example, officers perform daily telephone "beat checks" with community leaders. To some cops that may sound like a pain. But others like it. At least one officer on this department makes the calls from home, even if he is on sick leave. Another department directs officers to stop at homes with moving vans out front, to distribute police business cards and welcome new residents to the neighborhood.

Other departments, however, are finding success in acknowledging that COP policing moves at a different speed than radio-driven patrol work and that both types of policing deserve support.

The Phoenix Program

In the early 1980s, the Phoenix Police Department experimented with a business-centered community policing effort. Over the years, it grew to include not only business owners, but property owners, tenants, special interest groups, and neighborhood associations. "In our department, the decision to go to community-based policing was not an issue that was grabbed by our management team and shoved down our throats," says R.C. "Jake" Jacobsen, president of the Phoenix Law Enforcement Association, a police union that represents 2,500 uniformed officers.

Jacobsen, a 28-year veteran of the Phoenix PD, cites the Phoenix experience as a model for other agencies that want patrol officers to embrace community-oriented policing programs. "Community policing has to have complete buy-in from the people who are going to implement the program: street officers."

In Phoenix, each precinct squad is assigned a Community Action Officer (CAO), who serves as the direct point-of-contact person for neighborhood residents and others. Each squad also fields a Neighborhood Enforcement Team (NET), which actually implements crime-fighting or crime-prevention activities. Each team is comprised of six to seven uniformed officers, plus a sergeant.

Phoenix patrol officers were involved in the COP process via union representatives, who helped craft CAO and NET job descriptions, helped create a testing process, and monitor seniority and other fairness issues associated with the new positions. Patrol officers and detectives are encouraged to use NET as a resource for expanded investigations, follow-up monitoring, and in-the-field patrol backup.

The Phoenix PD's NET activities are wide ranging. They include surveillance, sting operations, extensive witness interviewing, and narcotics buy-bust campaigns. They also include such community-oriented policing projects as conducting classes on how to form a neighborhood association, teaching neighbors how to recognize drug houses, and educating people about how they can prevent auto theft.

"[The Phoenix program] has the potential for making the patrol officer's job a little easier," Jacobsen says. "If patrol officers rolling on a radio call notice that the burglary they are responding to is the fourth burglary in this week [in the area], they know where to go with it. They contact the CAO, and know someone is going to look into it."

Moreover, ties forged with community groups in Phoenix-the fifth-largest city in the nation-continue long after neighborhood meetings and crime-prevention classes are over.

"It's an amazing thing, to go to our city council meetings and see these community leaders fighting for police, standing with me to keep police programs that positively affect their neighborhoods," Jacobsen says. "If they didn't feel their voice was being heard, we wouldn't see the kind of support we see in Phoenix."

Phoenix PD management also acknowledges that comprehensive community-based policing strategies move at an entirely different speed than time-sensitive call-and-response patrol work.

"There will always be that demand for immediate response," Jacobsen says. "You try to approach everything from community-based policing standards, but the reality is if you're trying to work on quality-of-life issues and involving the community, you have to take a longer-term approach.

"Some problems you can solve in a week; some will take longer. That has nothing to do with response time. That's just the way it's understood here."

Geographical Policing

When the Boise (Idaho) Police Department decided to institutionalize community policing practices, it moved from a traditional, time-based policing model to a geography-based one and divided the city into 10 geographic service areas.

Each region has its own Neighborhood Contact Officer (NCO), who is located at conveniently placed area substations and is part of a larger Neighborhood Service Team (NST) comprised of sworn officers and civilians. The teams provide in-the-field investigations and other services tailored to needs in specific regions of the Pacific Northwest's third-largest city.

Earlier this year [2005], the NST system swung into action to combat an area vandalism spree that caused $20,000 in damaged property over a two-week period. The effort involved not just property-crimes detectives, but also school resource officers, crime-prevention and bike-patrol officers and, of course, vigilant neighborhood residents.

The culprits, a handful of baseball-bat-wielding juvenile males who bashed vehicles and windows as they drove past, were eventually identified and arrested.

Nothing New

Perhaps the aspect of community-oriented policing that irritates patrol officers the most is that it gives bureaucrats and administrators credit for common sense police work. The problem, according to community policing advocates, is that the patrol programs of some police agencies have prevented cops from acting on their instincts and communicating better with the people they serve.

"True community policing is what law enforcement was doing, without calling it that, 50 to 60 years ago," notes Boise PD Capt. William L. Bones. "When we got into cars, we tried to become more and more efficient with officers. It became all about how many calls can we get to and that has taken away the interaction with people. The idea behind community policing is to build that back up, and to help people take responsibility for their own neighborhoods."

Boise PD recognizes that laying the foundation for effective community policing-networking with housing development authorities, school officials, sanitation workers, social-service providers who work with specialty populations like the homeless and immigrant refugees, and other groups-takes time, says COPS unit Capt. Jim Kerns.

"Our NCOs have the ability to work with all the resources we have in the city to prevent and mitigate return calls for service," Kerns says. "The people of this city love their NCOs and would not want to see those people go away. And patrol officers would not want to see them go away, either, because they help solve the long-term problems that go along with our job. They handle the problems you can't handle in one call."

Bringing to Surface Good Cops

It has always been a mystery to many police investigators as to why bad cops are protected by good cops in view of the fact that if during an investigation it is found that the good cop witnessed a criminal act and covered it up, he or she would be prosecuted along with the bad cop.

Keeping silent is not an escape from the criminal or unethical act being investigated. It is an invitation to become a part of the act which can result in severe consequences.

Fortunately, in the late 1990s the "blue wall of silence" in hundreds of police departments across America began to crumble as community policing began to impact the way police officers performed their duties and how they interacted with each other.

Community policing brings to surface good cops who are tired of being stigmatized and stereotyped as being bad cops because of the unlawful and reckless behavior of the few cops who compromise their integrity.

Steven L. Rogers,
Proven Strategies for Effective
Community Oriented Policing, *2008.*

Manpower Issues

One agency that addressed manpower issues up front was the Suffolk County (N.Y.) Police Department, which services 1.1 million people in southeast New York.

"First, you have to define community policing for your particular community because it means different things for different communities," says Suffolk County Lt. Ted Nieves. "We realized right away, due to the size of our police district, that we had a lot of different needs for different areas, which is why we decentralized the community policing effort-each precinct commander could do what he saw fit."

Suffolk County's Community Oriented Police Enforcement (COPE) officers are assigned to precincts, and are responsible for activities in that specific geographic area. Like Boise and Phoenix PD community officers, they generate intelligence, solicit suggestions, and respond to complaints from a variety of sources, including patrol officers.

COPE officers also work to determine whether another, non-police agency, can best handle an issue. For example, each township has its own noise ordinance, and code enforcement officers are empowered to investigate, document violations, and issue citations. Police officer presence is not necessary.

"The [patrol] officers do get satisfaction from being freed up from these chronic problems on a daily basis," Nieves said. "It gives them an ability to deal with more serious crimes and root out some of the more 'heavy' crimes in the community."

More than Just Public Relations

However a police department decides to implement COP principles, one piece of advice remains the same, from small Minnesota farm towns to exploding Sunbelt mega-cities. "I think some police departments get misled when they don't have a full understanding of community policing, and see it primarily as community relations," says Benson, the former Flint PD deputy chief. "I'm a great believer in real community policing, not just handing out lollipops and hotdogs and not merely riding a bike or walking around a neighborhood. I'm talking about having geographic ownership, where the officer 'owns' his or her own beat, and the citizens 'own' their officer."

"We ought to take a hard look at what we are doing to make the community safer, and how much of the [publicity] 'show' can we take out of it," agrees CLEAT's DeLord. "Start by sitting down with the people who are out there every day. If you just create it up on the Fifth Floor [in the police commissioner's office], and it never makes it out to the stations, and is just announced, how effective is that going to be?"

| *"Overall, there was no statistical evidence that the [community-policing] program is associated with reductions in crime and violence."*

Community Policing May Not Reduce Crime

Jeremy M. Wilson and Amy G. Cox

Jeremy M. Wilson and Amy G. Cox assert in the following viewpoint that community-policing programs may not effectively reduce crime. In their analysis of a program implemented in Oakland, California, Wilson and Cox argue that the evidence does not support lowered crime levels. The authors present four possible explanations for their findings: (1) the program is ineffective; (2) their analysis does not capture other positive impacts of the program; (3) the program increased the reporting of crime, which counteracts crime reductions; and (4) the program faces implementation challenges, limiting its effectiveness. Wilson is an associate professor at Michigan State University's School of Criminal Justice and adjunct behavioral scientist at the Rand Corporation, a nonprofit policy research institute. Cox is a social scientist at Rand.

As you read, consider the following questions:

1. What is one explanation that Wilson and Cox offer that community-policing efforts do not translate into crime reductions?

2. As claimed by the authors, what can particularly hinder the implementation of community-policing programs among police officers?

3. What policy recommendation do Wilson and Cox provide for staffing community-policing programs?

Increases in violent crime in the early 2000s caused a great deal of concern among Oakland, California, residents and policymakers. In response, in November 2004, Oakland voters passed a ballot measure that created the Violence Prevention and Public Safety Act (also known as Measure Y), which provides $19.9 million per year for violence-prevention programs, 63 new police officers focused on community and neighborhood policing services, and an independent evaluation of the measure.

This report summarizes RAND's assessment of Measure Y–funded community-policing efforts through September 2008, expanding on the first-year process—or implementation—analysis and examining the effectiveness of community policing as implemented through the problem-solving officer (PSO) program. To conduct the analysis, we relied on four sources of information: (1) a Web-based survey of PSOs; (2) an assessment of PSO deployment data used to summarize the deployment, stability, and coverage of the PSOs; (3) official crime statistics from January 1, 1998, through April 30, 2008, used to form two crime measures for each PSO beat—violent crime and property crime—which, in turn, were used as outcome variables in interrupted time series analyses; and (4) semistructured interviews and focus groups with Oakland Police Department (OPD) staff.

Four Possible Explanations

Much progress has been made in implementing the PSO program in the second evaluation year, but such progress has not been associated with a reduction in violent or property crime. Overall, there was no statistical evidence that the PSO program is associated with reductions in crime and violence.

There are four possible explanations: (1) the program is not effective; (2) there are positive outcomes that the evaluation does not capture; (3) the program is associated with an increased propensity to report crime, thus off-setting crime reductions; or (4) implementation challenges preclude the program's ability to be effective. It is plausible that the efforts of the PSOs do not directly translate into crime reductions. There could be many reasons for this. For instance, the program theory could be flawed such that the specific actions of the PSOs, even when successful, are unrelated to crime prevention. Alternatively, it is possible that the work of a single PSO, while successful, is simply not sufficient to affect crime levels. This suggests a "dosage" problem and perhaps the need for more PSOs to realize a measurable reduction in crime. While it is entirely possible that PSOs do not impact crime, we cannot make such a determination with any degree of certainty, given current implementation challenges that undermine the ability of PSO deployment to affect property and violent crime rates, even if the problem-solving that is being conducted is successful. This will be more discernible in the future, assuming that the implementation of the PSO program improves.

Possible Shortcomings of the Analysis

The second possible explanation is that the evaluation did not capture the ultimate success of problem-solving efforts. Our analysis considered indexes of violent and property crime. It is possible that effects could be detected using other official statistics, such as individual crime or disorder measures, or even measures based on stakeholder perceptions, such as resident assessment of problem-solving efforts, fear of crime, or quality of life in the beat. Because Measure Y's overarching goal is to reduce crime and violence, the city's interest in assessing the impact of the PSOs on index crime, PSOs' ability to address problems theoretically and empirically related to crime, and the greater likelihood for index crime to be reported—broad measures used to assess PSOs' ultimate effectiveness in addressing these issues—figured heavily in our analysis. However, given the broad and diverse work of PSOs, the PSO program could be associated with positive outcomes pertaining to individual and intermediate outcomes that contribute to the ultimate reduction of violence but do not do so directly.

Not Enough Statistical Power

It is also possible that the outcome models estimated did not have enough statistical power to detect small or moderate effect sizes in the outcome variables. In beats where the PSO was deployed for a shorter period, the statistical power to detect a program effect is smaller because there are fewer post-deployment observations on which to estimate an effect. This potential problem can be addressed in future assessments by replicating these models after the PSOs have been working in their communities for longer periods, thereby creating a larger postdeployment sample.

The third explanation is that the success of PSOs resulted in an increased likelihood to report crime, thereby offsetting statistical reductions. Some support for this comes from the PSO survey results: Nearly half of the PSOs believed that community faith in the police and individual willingness to report crime have increased since their deployment. Unfortunately, it is impossible to determine with any degree of certainty the extent to which changes in crime reporting offset actual crime reductions achieved by the PSOs.

Implementation Challenges

The final explanation—that implementation challenges may preclude the ability of the PSO program to demonstrate success (assuming that it is effective) at this point—seems the most probable. Despite much progress in the problem-solving unit during this evaluation year, key implementation issues remain that could jeopardize problem-solving effectiveness: (1) the amount of problem-solving coverage that each beat receives, (2) the need for PSOs to "team up" on problem-solving in each other's beats, (3) the number of problems a given PSO addresses at any one time (an average of 32), (4) limited collaboration outside OPD, and (5) the instability of PSO assignments.

A few management issues also surfaced that could hinder the implementation and ultimate effectiveness of the PSO program—issues that point to the incentives that PSOs perceive with regard to their positions. In particular, some PSOs do not feel that they are evaluated accurately, and some do not desire to remain in their current positions. The final management issue pertains to the fact that documentation of PSO efforts is not standard or consistent across geographic areas, which may impede the ability of PSO commanders to monitor PSO activities, thereby limiting their ability to oversee and facilitate their efforts while also raising questions about the ability of PSO commanders to evaluate PSOs consistently. It should also be noted that the effectiveness of individual PSOs will likely increase as they gain more PSO experience, particularly if they remain assigned to a single beat where they can build strong community partnerships. Those responding to the survey had, on average, about eight years of experience as police officers and two years of experience as PSOs.

Policy Implications

These findings suggest the following policy recommendations: (1) assess the adequacy of staffing to determine the extent to which OPD needs additional staff or whether some other kind of reallocation of resources might improve problem-solving; (2) create a uniform problem-tracking system and monitor problem-solving efforts to promote problem management and evaluation; (3) actively consider ways to stabilize the PSO assignments and work with communities to soften transitions when they occur; (4) maximize stakeholder involvement and the use of existing resources, given that community participation in the problem-solving process continues to be less than ideal; (5) maximize incentives for PSOs with the goal of improving productivity and reducing attrition, thereby contributing to PSO stability, problem-solving effectiveness, and improved police-community relations; and (6) find ways to leverage Measure Y dollars to equip the officers with vehicles as quickly as possible.

"*[Neighborhood Watch] is directed to . . . act in relationship with police rather than neighbors.*"

Neighborhood Watch Groups Do Not Increase Safety

Jonathan Simon

In the following viewpoint, Jonathan Simon criticizes neighborhood watch groups and their putative protection of public safety. In light of the death of Trayvon Martin—an African American teenager shot by George Zimmerman, an armed neighborhood watch member—Simon maintains that these groups are motivated to enforce the law through the fear of crime and will inevitably cause grave harm. Unlike the other ways citizens participate in criminal justice, a neighborhood watch mobilizes its members to act as the police rather than as peers of their fellow citizens, the author argues. Simon is the Adrian A. Kragen Professor of Law and the director of the Center for the Study of Law and Society at the University of California, Berkeley.

As you read, consider the following questions:

1. What are the dynamics of neighborhood watch that potentially suppress crime, in the author's view?

2. What does Zimmerman reflect about neighborhood watch, in the author's opinion?

3. How does Simon characterize young African American males like Martin?

The killing of teenager Trayvon Martin earlier this month [in February 2012], in Sanford, Florida, has inflamed classic concerns about racism and criminal justice (especially in the South) as well as criticism of Florida's "stand your ground law"; a gun rights law that has expanded the circumstances under which self-defense may be raised in many states. Less noted has been the role of Neighborhood Watch [NW], a program launched by the National Association of Sheriffs in the 1970s with the objective of increasing the role of citizens in local crime prevention. Much beloved by criminologists and politicians alike, Neighborhood Watch is credited with reducing crime and improving police-citizen relations in many communities since the first trial program was run in Seattle in the mid-1970s. Trayvon Martin's death points to a darker side of Neighborhood Watch, one that may be unintended but predictable.

Trayvon Martin, a 17-year-old African-American high school student from Miami, was visiting with his father and his father's fiancé in the racially diverse suburb of Orlando when the shooting took place. The apparent killer, George Zimmerman, a 28-year-old of mixed Anglo-White/Latin American parentage had been very active in what was at best an informal neighborhood watch group (reports suggest he made over 50 calls to the police in the past several months). Zimmerman called the police to report suspicions about Trayvon (who was in fact walking home from a convenience store with a bag of candy and an ice tea while talking to his girlfriend on his cell phone). He apparently told police that Trayvon assaulted him and that he used his gun in self-defense, leading to a police decision not to arrest or charge Zimmerman in Martin's death. Public outrage built after the case received attention from the national media, including *New York Times* columnist Charles Blow last week. . . . Demonstrations have sparked appointment of a special prosecutor in Florida and widespread concern about Zimmerman's use of his weapon. There has been widespread debate about whether the killing plausibly fits the criteria intended by the "stand your ground" laws.

As a crime-prevention strategy, NW combines several potentially crime-suppressive dynamics, including facilitating quicker and more effective police response, deterring potential offenders through the observation of active and alert guardians, and altering the perceived opportunities for crime through routine activities like removing accumulating newspapers at the door of a home whose residents are away. The most recent meta-analysis of research on NW in both the US and the UK is modestly supportive of the proposition that neighborhood watch groups can reduce crime in their areas (with roughly half the communities studied showing some crime reduction and 12 of 18 empirical studies showing statistically significant differences between neighborhood watch covered areas and those without. According to the same study 27 percent of the British population and fully 40 percent of the US population live in a neighborhood in which some form of NW operates. . . .

"Governing Through Crime"

As a social formation, NW is also a vehicle for promoting law enforcement as a kind of citizenship project to which individual citizens are invited not only to support but to adopt. As such, it is a crucial expression of what I have called "governing through crime" and what [sociology and law professor David] Garland calls the "culture of control". Historically, citizens did participate in criminal justice as jurors, and as well as in the *posse comitatus* powers associated with citizen arrest. Neither approximates the distinctive political subjectivity mod-

eled by NW. As a juror, the citizen sits as a peer of the accused, not the police. Even as a member of a posse, the citizen acts as a peer of a fellow citizen who has raised the hue and cry against a trackable felon, a legal relationship that goes back to Norman England and, according to an article by renowned 20th century criminologist Sam Bass Warner, persisted in the US as a significant part of law enforcement in rural areas as late as the 1940s. . . . The Neighborhood Watch subject, in contrast, is mobilized to extend and supplement existing police forces in urban and suburban areas. Rather than being limited to pursuit of a fleeing felon, whose criminality has been witnessed by a neighbor, the political subject mobilized by NW is directed to attend to the quotidian [everyday] world of micro disorders and to act in relationship with police rather than neighbors.

Considering the role of race in this encounter suggests the continuities and differences with the Jim Crow [racial segregation] era. If mass incarceration is the New Jim Crow in [law professor] Michelle Alexander's formulation . . . it is because it is a legal structure that is also a racial order but not because it carries the same beliefs or mentalities about race on an either conscious or unconscious basis. Zimmerman is unlikely· to turn out to be some postmodern equivalent of Mississippi's Milam brothers who tortured and murdered 14 year-old- Emmet Till, an African American teen visiting his Misissippi family from Chicago in 1955 (the incident helped galvanize northern public opinion for federal enforcement of civil rights laws in the South in the year after *Brown v. Board of Education* was decided . . .).

Anchored in the Fear of Crime

Zimmerman, whoever he turns out to be, is more likely to reflect a new kind of law and order subject constituted by programs like Neighborhood Watch, and other cultural expressions of the war on crime, than the traditional racialized vigilante or racist neighborhood lynch mob member of the sort that afflicted Mississippi or even parts of Brooklyn and Queens as late as the 1980s. Till's banter with a married white woman in 1955 affronted the racialized Jim Crow honor code of the murderers. Zimmerman's lethal violence seems to have been activated by a different set of nonetheless racialized codes which Trayvon traduced [violated], one in which African American young men wearing hoodies are presumed to be cruising for criminal opportunities and should be prepared to perform their innocence visibly at all times (and not be distracted talking to their girlfriends). Zimmerman drove his SUV around his gated community, gun, and cell phone at his side not to enforce a racial order in which miscegenation [interracial marriage] is the gravest moral breach (indeed he was the product of a mixed racial marriage), but to enforce a civil order anchored in fear of crime in which fitting a racialized risk profile is a breach that can cost a young man his life.

> "It's highly unusual, and highly discour-
> aged, for a neighborhood watch to be
> armed."

Neighborhood Watch Groups Should Not Be Armed

Michael Rubinkam

*In the following viewpoint, Michael Rubinkam claims that mem-
bers of neighborhood watch groups should not carry weapons,
along with not confronting a suspicious individual or attempting
to stop a crime. The impulse to step in, the author explains,
grows strong during crime waves, when residents' frustrations
flare up. Rubinkam encourages members to call the police and
not intervene, as their lack of training can result in their own
victimization. While the effectiveness of neighborhood watch
groups is debated, he points out that the programs do increase
the sense of safety. Rubinkam is a reporter for the Associated
Press.*

As you read, consider the following questions:

1. What are neighborhood watch groups designed for, in
   Rubinkam's view?

2. What other ways can violent incidences involving neighborhood watch groups be prevented, according to the author?

3. Why do most neighborhood watch groups not last, in Kenneth J. Novak's view, as cited by Rubinkam?

Neighborhood watch groups were designed to be the eyes and ears of police—passively observing what they see and reporting back to law enforcement—not to enforce the law themselves.

Most neighborhood watches follow the rules, and confrontations are rare. But after the killing of unarmed black teenager Trayvon Martin in a Florida gated community, criminal justice experts say police departments and watch groups need to make sure volunteers do not take matters into their own hands.

"First thing: You do not engage. Once you see anything, a suspicious activity, you call the number that the police department has given you," said Chris Tutko, director of the Neighborhood Watch program at the National Sheriffs' Association, which launched the neighborhood watch concept 40 years ago as a response to rising crime.

Tutko said he was flabbergasted to learn about a watch captain's shooting of the 17-year-old Martin last month [in February 2012] in Sanford, Fla. Civil rights groups have demanded the arrest of the captain, George Zimmerman, who has said he shot Martin in self-defense. The Justice Department has opened a civil rights investigation.

Tutko said it's highly unusual, and highly discouraged, for a neighborhood watch to be armed.

"You do not carry a weapon during neighborhood watch," he said flatly. "If you carry a weapon, you're going to pull it."

Tens of thousands of watches have been formed across the United States over the decades. Some patrol gritty urban neighborhoods where volunteers walk a beat; others monitor sparsely populated areas with houses that are miles apart.

Contrary to the Idea of Neighborhood Watch

Regardless of location, the message from law enforcement is always the same: Do not intervene. Do not try to be a hero. Leave the crime-fighting to the police.

"We don't want to see somebody taking the law into their own hands," said Philadelphia police Sgt. Dennis Rosenbaum.

But the impulse can be strong, especially during a crime wave. In one Philadelphia neighborhood where vandals have been slashing tires for several months, residents are "fed up, frustrated," said Christina Hewitt, 23, whose mother has had her car targeted eight times since November.

Hewitt, who went to a neighborhood watch meeting Tuesday night with other residents and Philadelphia police, said the shooting in Florida was a topic of discussion.

Police, she said, told the residents "that's what they want to prevent."

Violent incidents involving neighborhood watch volunteers are rare but not unheard of. In 2009, two armed neighborhood watch volunteers in Bluffdale, Utah, got into a dispute; one took out his gun and shot the other, paralyzing him.

Background checks can weed out convicted felons and other people who obviously don't belong in neighborhood watches. After that, police departments that work with watch groups, as well as the organizations themselves, have to remain vigilant to make sure that volunteers are doing what they're supposed to.

"It was designed to be an extra set of eyes for the police because they cannot be everywhere all the time. But actually acting on it with vigilantism is completely askew to what the idea of neighborhood watch is," said Kenneth J. Novak, a

Watch Members Have No Police Powers

Patrol members should be trained by law enforcement. It should be emphasized to members that they do not possess police powers and they shall not carry weapons or pursue vehicles. They should also be cautioned to alert police or deputies when encountering strange activity. Members should never confront suspicious persons who could be armed and dangerous.

National Sheriffs' Association,
Neighborhood Watch Manual, *2005.*

criminal justice professor at the University of Missouri–Kansas City who has studied community policing and neighborhood watches.

Volunteers should resist the urge to intervene, Tutko said, even if they happen to see a crime in progress, because they lack training and may become victims themselves. He tells trainees that "you do what you can, when you can, as much as you can, but if you cross the line, everybody loses."

Intangible Benefits

Scholars say that while watch groups primarily act as deterrents and feed information to the police, they may provide more intangible benefits, too, like improving neighborhood cohesion and giving residents a sense of security.

The authors of a 2008 Justice Department review concluded there was "some evidence that Neighborhood Watch can be effective in reducing crime," but said that while some programs work as intended, others work less well or not at all.

Often started as a response to persistent crime, they can be a challenge to keep alive once the initial threat fades—either the bad guy is caught or goes elsewhere—and residents turn their attention away.

"Most neighborhood watches don't last very long. They usually galvanize themselves around an incident, or a series of similar incidents, and then the momentum dies out relatively quickly. That's why it's not really an effective crime prevention strategy on a wide scale," Novak said.

Allentown, an eastern Pennsylvania city of about 100,000, has managed to keep its neighborhood watch system going since the mid-1970s, with more than 20 individual groups and hundreds of volunteers.

They are not armed, and there has never been an incident, said Assistant Police Chief Joe Hanna.

"We tell them that we are the police, that if you see a crime in progress, get on the phone and call 911. We'll be there promptly, and let us handle the dangerous side of it," Hanna said. "The last thing we want is for them to put themselves in harm's way" or hurt someone else.

Periodical and Internet Sources Bibliography

The following articles have been selected to supplement the diverse views presented in this chapter.

Amanda Codispoti	"Community Cop: Acting Police Chief Chris Perkins Said He Knows Roanoke and Its Crime Problems and Wants to Build on the Community Policing Programs He Helped Launch," *Roanoke (VA) Times*, July 25, 2010.
John Dixon III and Esther Hyatt	"Decreasing Urban Crime," *FBI Law Enforcement Bulletin*, March 2011.
Mick Dumke	"Community Policing Is Caught in a Cross-Fire," *New York Times*, January 9, 2011.
Chris Foreman	"Crime Watches Increasing; Police Cite Their Effectiveness," *Pittsburgh Tribune-Review*, December 11, 2011.
Justin Gabbard	"Watchmen," *Tablet Magazine*, May 26, 2011. www.tabletmag.com.
Matthew Kemeny	"Harrisburg Puts Hope in Community Policing," *Patriot-News* (Central Pennsylvania), September 16, 2010. www.pennlive.com.
Donald Lambro	"Disobeying the Neighborhood Watch Rule to 'Stay in Your Car,'" TownHall.com, July 24, 2013. www.townhall.com.
Daniel Luzer	"Volunteer Security and the Rise of the Neighborhood Watch," *Pacific Standard*, July 23, 2013.
Bernard K. Melekian	"The Office of Community Oriented Policing Services," the *Police Chief*, March 2011.
Samantha Nolan	"Neighborhood Watch in D.C.: Vigilance, Not Vigilantes," *Washington Post*, March 30, 2012.

OPPOSING
VIEWPOINTS®
SERIES

CHAPTER 3

How Can Community Policing Be Improved?

Chapter Preface

As a departure from traditional law enforcement, community policing calls for specialized training. "Community policing requires major internal changes, and it also requires rethinking the ways in which the department relates to other individuals and groups in the community," assert law enforcement experts Ron Sloan, Robert C. Trojanowicz, and Bonnie Bucqueroux. Although training is recommended for all levels of personnel—including non-sworn civilians—emphasis is placed on training line officers, who patrol the streets and directly interact with the community.

For effective community policing, line officers must be trained to leave their vehicles during free patrol time, which is essential in establishing relationships with local residents, business owners, and community leaders and encourage their cooperation in preventing crime or investigating incidents. "If academy trainees have been recruited with the understanding that they will be expected to leave their automobiles on free patrol time, then they will be more amenable to doing so once out on their own," maintain Sloan, Trojanowicz, and Bucqueroux. "Academy training can reinforce this expectation by pointing out how face-to-face contact is essential in gaining the trust of citizens, so that the officers can work with people on problem solving."

Line officers also rely on a host of skills to interact with the community and can benefit from training in other areas, from learning a new language to understanding the basics of psychology. "It requires little imagination to come up with an intriguing roster of classes," suggest Sloan, Trojanowicz, and Bucqueroux, "yet the question becomes how much training is both feasible and affordable." The experts acknowledge that, in the face of time and budget constraints, such education may have to take the form of self-study or come at the expense of other training. In the following chapter, the authors propose different ways in which community policing can be improved.

I "*Preserving community-oriented polic-*
ing . . . requires changes to traditional
outreach methods."

Community Policing Needs Various Sources of Support

Zach Friend and Rick Martinez

To preserve community policing amid spreading budget cuts, law enforcement agencies must reach out to various groups for support and seek creative ways to maintain these programs, argue Zach Friend and Rick Martinez in the following viewpoint. The authors recommend that police departments meet with community members to gain insight into their concerns and to build trust, establish relations with the influential media, develop rapport with elected officials to address budget and policy decisions, and implement innovative procedures to continue funding community policing programs. These resources, Friend and Martinez contend, can help bring in federal funding. Friend is principal administrative analyst and spokesman for the Santa Cruz Police Department in California. Martinez is a lieutenant in the Santa Cruz Police Department.

Zach Friend and Rick Martinez, "Preserving Community-Oriented Policing in a Recession," *PM Magazine*, vol. 92, no. 3, April 2010. Copyright © 2010 by International City/Country. All rights reserved. Reproduced by permission

As you read, consider the following questions:

1. Aside from empowering the community, what does community policing achieve for the police agency, as stated by Friend and Martinez?

2. What are the benefits of holding regular community meetings and participating in neighborhood meetings for police agencies, as described by the authors?

3. How to the authors address the concern that engaging with elected officials is a political move for police agencies?

Widespread budget cuts have forced cities and law enforcement agencies to do more with less. Many police departments are doing something that hasn't been on the radar for years: laying off cops. Cities such as Oakland, California, have considered reductions of more than 15 percent to the force while others have eliminated all prevention and education programs. Often during times of retraction, it is easy to go after programs that consume time and resources regardless of the tangible results they yield.

Yet, even with a need to slash budgets, the question remains: can police agencies actually *afford* to cut community-oriented policing programs? For the Santa Cruz, California, Police Department, with fewer than 100 sworn in a town of 56,000, its established community policing program saved the agency from having to lay off cops; a dilemma faced for the first time in more than 140 years.

What exactly is community-oriented policing? Simply stated: it is policing that focuses on prevention, partnerships, and establishing trust. It empowers members of the community to become stakeholders in their own safety. It also transforms the image of the agency for those who support it financially and otherwise—local elected officials, community members, and the federal government.

In July 2009, the U.S. Department of Justice awarded more than $1 billion in American Recovery and Reinvestment Act funding for the COPS [Community Oriented Policing Services] program. This money was specifically to hire, rehire, or retain officers—a three-year funding mechanism to insulate local law enforcement agencies against further budget cuts. But how does an agency tap into this type of funding? What mechanisms can an agency create to ensure that it is more likely to succeed when future funding opportunities arise? The first step is establishing a relationship with community organizations.

Establishing Community Relationships

Public safety is both a primary responsibility of local government and a core expectation of community members. Santa Cruz Mayor Cynthia Mathews points out that "it is essential that the agency actively engage with the community to expand public understanding of services and procedures, gain first-hand knowledge of community concerns and perceptions, and cultivate citizen involvement." This allows agencies to "create personal relationships, build trust, and demonstrate responsiveness. Building these relationships increases both the quality of the agency's work and public support."

Mary Miller, who is on the board of Santa Cruz's largest neighborhood organization, Santa Cruz Neighbors, says that establishing a relationship with the police can be simpler than many think: "Begin by identifying several community-minded individuals who are interested in building strong ties among the neighbors and with law enforcement regarding issues such as a neighborhood watch program. These individuals can then reach out to other individuals and other neighborhoods and, with local law enforcement, begin to build the infrastructure for a strong community policing and neighborhood-involved program." Miller states that the framework for the policing model would be threefold: informational meetings to introduce beat officers to their area of responsibility, educational meetings to address specific localized problems, and management-level meetings to bring together community leaders and police management from a more macro perspective.

Often when you establish these community policing principles, such as holding regularly scheduled community meetings in each beat or participating actively in neighborhood group meetings, you will discover tangential benefits. Elected officials usually attend these events and can be significant allies in framing your image within the community. In addition, local businesses (often the lifeblood of a city tax base) are eager to partner with police agencies that emphasize this type of outreach.

"Strong, proactive, and positive relationships with the local business community and other key stakeholders ensure that local law enforcement are constantly in touch with the issues impacting local citizens," comments Kris Reyes, president of Kris Reyes Consulting, a Santa Cruz-based full-service communications and strategy firm. "It also humanizes the department in the eyes of most people. Officers become our friends, neighbors, and colleagues."

Reyes notes that the Santa Cruz Police Department has worked hard over the past few years to build relationships with all sectors of the business community. In turn, these relationships ensure that open lines of communication exist between both sides. "As a result, it is very easy to communicate with the department regarding issues that impact the local business community. Most importantly, the police do a great job of listening to local business owners and finding creative solutions to challenging issues."

Building Relationships with the Media

Regardless of what you may instinctively think, law enforcement and the media have a lot in common. Many journalists see their profession as a calling and as an essential element in public service. Journalists, much like cops, receive a significant amount of pressure and scrutiny from the public. But beyond the similarities, it is essential to build positive relationships with the media for two other reasons: their influence on public opinion and their influence on public policy.

There is no question that implementing a successful community-based policing model will be reflected in more community-oriented coverage. After all, when you speak to the media you are really speaking to the community at large. Mayor Mathews points out that media coverage of public safety issues exerts a powerful influence on public perception of community needs and police performance. The Santa Cruz Police Department has worked hard, through the establishment of a public information officer (PIO) position and media training for management staff, to communicate its message to the community effectively.

Creating a PIO will allow an agency to centralize its message and focus fully on communicating information to the public and media. This position, often an assignment within the department, will remove a great burden from the supervisory staff who are usually tasked with this function. In addition, the PIO will take the responsibility at crime scenes, allowing patrol staff to deal with the issue at hand.

"The American political system is very fragmented—by design," according to Joe Ferrara, associate dean, Georgetown Public Policy Institute. "Political power is constantly shifting, vertically and horizontally." He points out that community groups and the media play a large role in these ongoing shifts. "Public safety—probably more than most policy areas—operates in an environment of constant community and media scrutiny." In turn, he believes law enforcement agencies need to be sensitive to this dynamic and understand how community groups and the media can affect public perceptions.

Police Are by Default Political

Police agencies are quick to fall victim to the belief that engaging with elected officials somehow equates to being political. But the truth is that when you are the highest-profile department in a city government structure and you take the largest chunk of the budget you are by default a political organization. There is no reason to stand on the sidelines while political decisions are being made.

After all, the community holds elected officials accountable for all public services, including policing. Why would you allow elected officials to make budgetary decisions that can directly impact your operations or form opinions about the efficacy of your agency without taking the time to educate them? "In order to respond to public concerns and make sound decisions about public policy and budgets, elected officials need to have a solid, honest understanding of departmental strengths and challenges," according to Santa Cruz Mayor Cynthia Mathews. "This can only happen if there are solid relationships and open communication between the department and electeds, based on trust and shared goals."

How would a police agency develop these relationships? The key element is to be proactive and to invest a significant amount of time to establish a dialogue before there is a crisis or a major budgetary decision. Reach out to each of your local city council members, and assume that they do not have a strong understanding of your department. Mayor Mathews counsels that, whether or not you perceive certain elected officials will be supportive, you must take time to get to know each one individually.

For example, the mayor says, "What are their values, life experience, and background that will shape their perceptions of public safety issues and performance?" Departments need to "maximize the opportunities for interaction through proactive invitations to participate in roll call, departmental events, ride-alongs, and community meetings." Consequently, anything that develops background knowledge about your agency or creates a sense of shared mission and personal relationships will in the long run benefit the relationship with elected officials and ultimately your department.

Preserving Community Policing

In healthier economic times, the Santa Cruz Police Department staffed a community services unit with a manager, supervisor, three patrol officers, and three community service officers. During those fully staffed years, the unit was hosting or attending weekly community meetings and hosting three citizen police academies, one of which was designed solely for Spanish speakers. Today's budget constraints have forced the elimination of the unit. It did not, however, eliminate the department's community outreach.

The police department's community policing efforts are overseen by a handful of managers working out of the patrol division. Beats within the city have been divided into areas of responsibility for police managers in order to ensure there is a single point of contact for community members. To preserve some semblance of community policing in the department, managers partner with community groups to help conduct outreach efforts, mobilize neighborhoods, and facilitate community meetings. The partnership amounts to an ad hoc community policing partnership that has many strengths and replaces (although imperfectly) the former fully funded program.

Besides the obvious cost savings, the use of community groups to continue the community policing message helps to maintain a constant level of communication and partnership with the whole community. And, as many agencies transition from a traditional field training officer program to a police training officer (PTO) program, innovation gleaned from the PTO program can be integrated easily into the ad hoc community policing partnership.

With the national call for citizens to step up and participate in public service, now is the time for community policing
agencies to use the newly emerging resource. Agencies like the
Santa Cruz Police Department, struggling to financially support a viable community policing program, are finding community policing partnerships to be the most effective way to
maintain the level of service residents expect. The program
has also demonstrated a commitment to the community-
oriented policing philosophy that has greatly aided the department in receiving federal grant funds and insulated the police
from local cuts.

Preserving community-oriented policing in a recession can
be accomplished, but it requires changes to traditional outreach methods. Methods suggested in this article can be broken into four steps:

- Meet with community groups.

- Establish a PIO to improve media relations.

- Meet with elected officials; proactively invest this time
  before a crisis occurs.

- Implement creative procedures and policy changes that
  maintain community-oriented policing practices.

Without question, police agencies are being forced to make
exceptionally difficult decisions during these times of tight
budgets. Santa Cruz's emphasis on maintaining community
policing partnerships has actually brought in financial benefits, however; in 2009 the department was awarded nearly $2
million in federal COPS grants, preserving five positions slated
for layoffs. The city also has found that the department's relationship with the community has allowed for an environment
more amenable to bond measures and greater support for tax
increases that fund public safety.

Officers have also experienced a tangible improvement in
their general working relationship with the community as

they continue with community policing. Many officers report hearing "thank yous" more often from the community during their day-to-day patrols.

> "With feds and local cops increasing their collaborations and seeking funding to expand their joint investigations, we may be seeing the end of 'community policing' as we've known it."

How the Federal Government Is Killing Community Policing

Sudhir Venkatesh

Sudhir Venkatesh is a sociology professor at Columbia University in New York City. In the following viewpoint, he declares that federal support of local law enforcement agencies negatively impacts community policing. Although these partnerships have netted high numbers of arrests and convictions as well as enhanced the perception of safety in the short term, Venkatesh proposes that unlike federal agents, cops walking the beat primarily maintain relations and mediate with criminals, which allows them to informally defuse a range of situations and protect innocent citizens. However, such effective but cash-strapped enforcement is disappearing as federal funding and involvement increases, leaving a vacuum waiting to be filled by vigilantism, the author concludes.

As you read, consider the following questions:

1. Why do local police accept federal involvement with little resistance, in Venkatesh's view?

2. According to Venkatesh, what can happen to a police chief if federal agents and prosecutors seek high-profile arrests?

3. What examples does the author use to support his position that local police compete with federal agents for funding?

If you've ever watched a television series, like "Hill Street Blues" or "NYPD Blue," you are probably well acquainted with the mutual disdain between local and federal law enforcement. While the script for these shows was predictable, it was engrossing nonetheless. Cops were local bumpkins who policed on gut instinct, and whose ties to locals made corruption an ever-present danger. Feds were arrogant 'suits' who used wiretaps and hi-tech devices to drag in dozens at a time—cops included. When I recently joined the FBI in an advisory position—I spent two years visiting field offices around the country in an effort to understand how federal agents put together a case, and to gauge their impact on local public safety—such antagonism is exactly what I expected to find.

Instead, I saw a different drama, one that has received far less attention, but is no less compelling. Increasingly, across the country, the town cop who walks a beat and relies on trust with locals may be a thing of the past; your neighborhood police investigation is increasingly likely to be a federal initiative, built on cooperation between your local police department and Washington, DC. In fact, with feds and local cops increasing their collaborations and seeking funding to expand their joint investigations, we may be seeing the end of "community policing" as we've known it. In the short run, this has been a good thing, since crime has grown more complex and stiff federal penalties are often necessary deterrents. But in the long run, it's shaping up to be the biggest challenge to liberal governance and local autonomy that we've seen in some time.

Federal-local partnerships currently target a surprisingly wide range of crimes and it's hard to pinpoint the criteria determining the involvement of FBI, DEA, ICE and other Department of Justice officials in local matters. Sometimes the locals are out-matched, at other times multiple-jurisdictions require federal coordination, and on occasion, a federal prosecutor simply finds a racketeering case too good to pass up. It's almost always true, however, that the relationship is openly transactional. The feds bring gifts to the locals, in the form of cars, decent pay, and fancy surveillance gadgetry. In return the feds "rent" local cops (and the local knowledge they possess).

And the results can be impressive: For violent gang interdiction alone, the FBI's "Safe Streets" Taskforce has worked with police to net 55,000 arrests and 23,000 convictions. That is an extraordinary number given that the modern gangs are working out of prisons and communities that cut across the jurisdictions of local police departments—and sometimes national borders.

The arrests are not the only victories. In Chicago, I assessed the outcome of such so-called "taskforce"-style partnerships and the evidence was promising: Residents felt safer using public spaces, storeowners experienced less extortion, and even gang members exited their organizations at a greater rate after a federal operation—unlike the past, today's local-federal collaborations are well publicized. In the city's Southside communities, where a typical month now hosts several hundred incidents of gun violence, this is no trivial accomplishment. And, of course, with towns, counties, and states struggle to fund services, federal resources are that much more attractive. Everyone wants the feds.

It's worth remarking, however, that this marks an enormous shift in American policing. Federal taskforces pose a direct threat to community policing, the enforcement strategy based on the belief that public safety is strongest when local cops and local community leaders work hand-in-hand. For decades, this style of policing was the national model of crime prevention. It kept money in the hands of mayors, police chiefs, and the unions. The biggest domestic law enforcement initiative in the last 30 years—Bill Clinton's "Community Oriented Policing Services" (COPS) program, which funded 100,000 officers at a cost of $7.6 billion—was based on the community policing strategy.

But the COPS initiative, ultimately, did little to stop or solve crimes. (The Government Accountability Office attributed only a 1.3 percent of crime reduction to the program.) Indeed, there's reason to believe that community policing has become less effective as crime has become more complex. Criminals now routinely cross (state and international) borders, they work through prison networks even for local gang recruitment, and they are as likely as cops to draw on their own hi-tech tools. Local police in high crime areas simply couldn't keep up on their own, and were forced into essentially becoming war-time surgeons performing triage. They had to choose which crimes to follow, prioritizing only those conflicts most likely to unravel and harm innocents. And they could not follow any particular crime or criminal for very long.

Until, that is, someone gave them money to do more. Small wonder local police put up little resistance when federal agents asked to lease their staff. In police departments from Camden to Jacksonville to Oakland, where layoffs and restricted budgets have made classic daily beat patrols a luxury, the feds have deployed their technological arsenal—wiretaps, web scraping, voice and image recognition—to great effect. And necessity is breeding innovation. In the cities where taskforces dominate, policing is becoming unprecedentedly dynamic and nimble, involving police, when necessary, from a wide range of jurisdictions.

After reviewing the data on taskforce impacts on crime, it's hard not to admit that federal law enforcement deserves its preponderance of funding. In many ways, old-fashioned community policing was no longer getting the job done, and it needed a face lift. The traditional big city approach looks clunky in comparison.

But federal money is no panacea. The goals of beat policing and federal investigations are not always closely aligned. A dirty little secret of good policing is that cop and thug communicate more often than we think. In nearly 20 years of watching cops and criminals duel one another on inner-city streets, I've rarely heard a beat officer say their first priority is to *prevent* crime. Most often, they are intervening in order to put out fires before innocents get hurt. This means knowing what thug to call (or threaten) after a flare-up. So what happens when federal agents and prosecutors want high-profile arrests for racketeering or other federal crimes? The answer is that when a police chief accepts federal largesse, she may also have to accept federal priorities—even if they hurt her ability to maintain good relations on the street.

The city cops and police chiefs I met were hesitant to talk openly about this (and with so much money at stake, I wasn't expecting them to confess their grievances.) But local police are not naïve; they know that they are not just cooperating with the Feds, but competing with them. The Feds are getting a bigger share of funding, while they are forced to continually make layoffs. (President Bush was a game changer in this respect, in the way that he prioritized international terrorism; President Obama has continued the tradition, favoring funding of federal agencies over local departments. His $2.2 billon crime-fighting grant (2010) sounds impressive, but only 8 percent of the local police applications were honored, and only 10,000 cops were hired—a far cry from Clinton's efforts. 2011 funding for community policing was a paltry $111 million.)

But even if local police remain tight-lipped about these trends, it's our civic responsibility to recognize that even the best top-down policies can have unintended consequences. Reducing beat-style community policing creates a vacuum in local communities. A good cop spends far more time settling disputes informally than arresting people. From domestic violence to gangbanging, community policing can bring about timely, on-the-spot mediations and compromises where parties can go back into their corner and cool off. Though I saw a few FBI officers display this skill set, for the most part federal agents are too busy shuttling between crises to do this kind of work. Their solution is incarceration, which is a terribly ineffective means of creating daily public safety.

If you're wondering how these vacuums get filled, look no further than Sanford, Florida, where a gun-toting self-appointed neighborhood watchman shot and killed a young man he suspected of involvement in a crime. When it comes to the Guardian Angels or volunteer citizen patrols and block clubs, America's tradition of self-reliance deserves recognition. But the line between a citizen army and a vigilante force is often blurry.

Still, in the absence of community policing, communities of citizens will continue to try to solve their problems on their own. In Chicago, where a wave of gun violence is currently cresting, neighborhood residents have given up on calling 911, instead reaching out to work directly with local gangs when the cops aren't around. It's not inconceivable, of course, that they will soon simply find themselves calling 411 to get the number of their local FBI office.

> *"The success of [combining community policing and social services] is that it ... ensures that each of the main actors (cops, community leaders, and service providers) reads from the same script."*

On the Block

Chris Smith

Chris Smith is a writer and photographer based in California's San Francisco Bay Area. In the following viewpoint, Smith contends that programs combining community policing with social services effectively reduce crime. The two approaches alone are not effective in the hardest-hit neighborhoods, he explains, but the integration of counseling, job placement, and other resources with a local enforcement strategy has helped many at-risk youth change their lives. Citing outreach programs in Oakland, California, and around the country, Smith contends that not only have murders and shootings been cut dramatically, but repeat offenders have been taken off the streets.

Chris Smith, "On the Block," *American Prospect*, vol. 22, no. 1, January–February 2011, p. 6.

As you read, consider the following questions:

1. Why are policing and social services ineffective as separate approaches in the most troubled neighborhoods, according to Smith?

2. What statistics does the author provide for the success of Ceasefire, the first program to integrate community policing and social services?

3. What does Kevin Grant state regarding the uncertainty of alternative policing programs, as cited by Smith?

It's been raining and the San Francisco Giants are on TV, so the streets are quiet. We're cruising through East Oakland, one of the most violent parts of a violent city. A knot of drug dealers loiters in front of a housing project, and crackheads sit in folding chairs on the sidewalk. Two teenagers in hoodies saunter by; another weaves back and forth on a small bike. Anthony DelToro gestures toward them: "When you see youngsters like that, all in black, the majority of the damn time they got guns." He pauses. "This is Oakland—everybody got a gun."

DelToro, a 24-year-old East Oaklander who wears an extra-large white T-shirt and a Giants baseball hat, knows of what he speaks. He grew up in a Norteño gang neighborhood, sold coke, heroin, and weed and served stints totaling two-and-a-half years in county jails. He now leads a Street Outreach team of locals in their 20s to 40s—some are ex-gang members and drug dealers, some have lost loved ones to violence. The common denominator is that they all command respect on the street.

They don white jackets (inscribed with the words "For a Safer Oakland") and walk through rough neighborhoods four nights a week. Crime drops when they're on the job: from 20 percent in an East Oakland hotspot to 32 percent in West Oakland, according to a study done for the city by an independent auditor. Statistics, however, don't measure everything the outreach workers do. They negotiate truces, act as mentors, and offer criminals a future—that doesn't involve prison or death—through jobs, counseling, or a face-saving way to return to school. "We may not have the answer," DelToro says, "but we can lead them to the people who do."

There are only a dozen Street Outreach workers, but they play an outsize role in the city's fight against crime. They're not cops—far from it. Still, they are an integral part of Oakland's Lifeline program, the local iteration of an innovative alternative-policing strategy that has cut down on arrests and decreased homicides by up to 50 percent in cities nationwide by combining iron-fisted law enforcement with old-school "root causes" measures such as wraparound social services.

As it turns out, in the most troubled neighborhoods, neither approach works well in isolation. Aggressive policing alienates the communities it aims to help, and the sheer level of dysfunction in places like East Oakland can frustrate even the best social programs. The success of Lifeline is that it joins these elements and ensures that each of the main actors (cops, community leaders, and service providers) reads from the same script. As Kevin Grant, an elder street statesman who spent over a decade in a federal prison for selling drugs and now coordinates the city's violence-prevention network, puts it, "It's a tag-team effort."

The model was test run in Boston in 1996, at the tail end of the nation's crack epidemic. David Kennedy, then a researcher at Harvard and now a professor at John Jay College of Criminal Justice, and two colleagues noticed that less than 1 percent of the population was responsible for the majority of violence in most cities. They decided to concentrate on these high-volume criminals, many of whom were gang members. They designed a program in which a coalition of authorities, both legal and moral, told these apparent incorrigibles to quit killing and offered immediate job training and counseling if they did. If they refused to quit, the law came down on them—hard.

Operation Ceasefire, as it is known, was startlingly successful. Boston saw a 50 percent drop in murders. As Ceasefire spread to other cities, it became obvious that Boston wasn't a fluke. In Cincinnati, gang-related murders fell by half. In Stockton, California, a working-class city about 75 miles east of Oakland, gang-related youth homicides fell from 18 in 1997 to just one in 1998.

While the model focuses on curbing violence, it also tries to ensure its social-services work takes hold. (Outreach teams aren't used everywhere, but some cities have found them highly effective at both reducing violence and convincing offenders to accept help.) Kennedy now co-chairs the National Network for Safe Communities, of which Oakland and cities like Los Angeles and Chicago are a part.

Kennedy, who first published his ideas in [the *American Prospect*] (see "Can We Keep Guns Away from Kids?" Summer 1994), co-founded the network to help cities adapt the Ceasefire model to their needs by offering technical assistance, research, and specialists to aid in the rollout. In Oakland, the NNSC is beginning to fine-tune the city's violence-prevention strategies and to research their effectiveness. These measures are essential for securing the necessary funding and institutional support to entrench the programs as official policy. Kennedy's intention is to "reset" the relationships between law enforcement and offenders by implementing the program everywhere it is needed. If that happens, he estimates, "it'll cut the homicide rate by half nationwide, maybe more."

Oakland certainly needs help. In 2009 it was ranked the nation's third most violent city, according to the publisher CQ Press, which analyzes the FBI's annual crime numbers and assigns an overall score for almost 400 cities. Oakland is a divided city, split between affluent hilltop neighborhoods and flatlands in which the poor scrape by, their streets patrolled by a police force often seen as an occupying army.

The city has experimented with what has become known as community policing. In criminal justice, that's often shorthand for an alternative enforcement strategy that puts police in close contact with the communities they serve, collaborating to prevent crime instead of reacting to it. Of course, as implemented across hundreds of jurisdictions, community policing has meant different things depending on the locale.

In Oakland, a dedicated beat officer works proactively with neighborhood crime-prevention groups on local concerns like prostitution and drug-dealing to ensure that each community has a fixed point of contact with the police. The policy has seen a number of false starts (one past police chief, for instance, didn't like the idea of his officers "going native"), but crime has dropped over the last few years.

Faced with a budget deficit of $30.5 million last summer, however, Oakland laid off 80 cops and more than half of its neighborhood service coordinators and reassigned its community-policing officers to patrol. More budget cuts and layoffs are likely.... The Oakland Police Department insists that community policing will continue, but it is unclear what it will look like.

Howard Jordan, Oakland's assistant chief of police, says that the department has trained its officers in preventive- and community-oriented policing, and that patrol officers will continue to tackle neighborhood problems when they have the time. "Our ideal is to make everyone a community-policing officer," he says. "It just depends on your definition of community policing."

Lifeline, which plans to hire more outreach workers, promises to fill some of the gaps in police presence. While Lifeline's work isn't community policing, it serves many of the same ends. Lifeline doesn't ask cops to become social workers, as the cliche goes; it just asks them to enforce the law more se-

Police Partnerships with Social Services

As one of the most ubiquitous public agencies, police departments can be a bridge between the communities they serve and other parts of government. Their position in municipal government offers the potential to leverage resources to which poor communities might not otherwise have access. As first responders—and one of the few agencies that operates 24 hours a day, 7 days a week—police have a greater capacity than other government agencies for intervening in communities and are in a unique position to reach families in crisis. Partnerships with social service agencies enhance police capacity to refer individuals to available resources and help social service agencies reach clients in need.

Liliokanaio Peaslee,
Police Policy and Research, *April 2009.*

lectively to avoid the indiscriminate crackdowns that anger communities, which frees police to concentrate on the worst offenders. The outreach workers help tamp down violence in the city's most volatile areas and connect young guys on the corners with the social services that provide a path out of the thug life. When all the parts work together, communities can reclaim their neighborhoods. So far, Lifeline's approach appears to be working.

Last spring, a police officer hand-delivered a letter to Erik Agreda, a 28-year-old repeat offender who lives in West Oakland, demanding he attend a meeting for habitual offenders at City Hall. This is known as the "call in," Lifeline's police-run component. Call-in participants are either on probation or on parole and possess lengthy rap sheets. Agreda was no exception. He had just finished his latest stint, 11 months for crack possession, in November 2009.

Agreda and 10 other men were summoned to a municipal conference room where they stared down a crowd of cops, U.S. attorneys, FBI agents, and neighborhood community leaders. Each speaker came at the subject from a different angle. The cops threatened prison time; the community leaders, which included relatives of crime victims, struck a more conciliatory tone. Their message was unmistakable: Stop the violence.

Agreda says he wasn't impressed by the tough talk: "I thought it was bullshit. They tried to scare us, saying they were going to hand our files to the feds."

Afterward, an outreach manager asked Agreda if he needed help with anything. Agreda was unemployed and shot back sarcastically, "Yeah, can you find me a job?"

"I meant it as a bluff," Agreda says. He probably would have forgotten about the offer of help, but the case manager followed up a few days later with an opening for a temporary position. Soon Agreda was sorting trash and recycling and loading trucks and building furniture for Pottery Barn and West Elm.

Agreda is trying to make the change stick. He's been out of prison for a year—his longest period of being a free adult—and trying to get off probation for the first time in seven years. "I've been in trouble most of my life," he says. "Usually it's seven months and I'm back in again. It's time to grow up."

Little hard data exists yet on Lifeline's effectiveness, but the preliminary evidence is encouraging. There have been 11 call-ins with 80 habitual offenders since November 2009.... Oakland's unemployment rate is 17 percent, and these men rank among the city's least employable, but nearly 30 percent have already found work. Close to 20 percent, meanwhile, are back in school. While 19 of the men have violated their parole or probation, only eight have committed new offenses, a 10 percent recidivism rate compared to the county-wide recidivism rate of 39 percent within the first year. Plus, only a handful of the new violations were violent, a minor miracle considering the group's history.

A similar trend has played out in Ghost Town, a mostly African American neighborhood in West Oakland. This pocket of empty storefronts and rundown bungalows has seen 149 shootings and killings since 2007, the third-highest total in the city. Before Lifeline became involved, the police regularly swept the neighborhood and made many arrests, but it wasn't enough. "Traditional police work hadn't done the job," Jordan says.

In 2008, the outreach teams began their work. The following year, police started the call-ins, zeroing in on the worst offenders. The violence has dropped sharply: Only nine of those 149 shootings and homicides occurred in the first seven months of 2010. "When we started this process, there were bodies on the streets," says Don Link, a former member of the city's Community Policing Advisory Board who chairs a neighborhood crime-prevention group. "Now shootings are the exception rather than the rule."

For all its promise, Lifeline is still evolving, and its future is uncertain. Oakland's politics are defined by fiefdoms that rarely agree on criminal-justice issues, and programs come and go with terrifying speed. There's no guarantee, for instance, that the next mayor, who takes office in January [2011], will continue to support Lifeline. Grant, the violence-prevention coordinator, has seen this process up close over the years. "You can have a perfect program," he says, "and it's working, but in two years they'll say, 'Oh, it's over with. There's a new mayor in town, and that was married to the old mayor so wipe it from the table.'" It can be frustrating, but he says he hopes the new administration, seeing Lifeline's success, will allow the program to grow.

Beyond crime statistics, Lifeline already has accomplished things that many Oaklanders would have thought unlikely, if not impossible. In its small-bore way the program is helping to bridge the divide between police and communities. Jordan was skeptical at first of working with ex-felons, but he's a believer now: "The outreach workers reach the hearts and minds of people who would never listen to us."

Back in West Oakland, Agreda says he's doing well, managing his family's gift store and raising his 3-year-old son. He remains skeptical about the call-in but admits that it pushed him in the right direction: "In a weird way, it served its purpose."

| "*Law enforcement [can] leverage social media to take community policing to another level.*"

Social Media Can Enhance Community Policing

Dan Alexander

Dan Alexander is the police chief of the Boca Raton, Florida, Police Services Department (BRPD). In the following viewpoint, Alexander suggests that social media technologies and platforms can enhance community policing. A law enforcement agency can use services such as Facebook, YouTube, and blogs to brand itself, reach out to the community, and define its role within it, he contends. Furthermore, with shrinking media coverage of crimes and arrests, an agency can inform citizens of such news through social media, Alexander asserts. This two-way communication is also a valuable tool during emergencies and disasters, he says, and the police can keep the community updated as situations or conditions develop through tweets and social media posts.

As you read, consider the following questions:

1. What does social media allow the BRPD to do in serving a fluctuating population, according to the author?

Dan Alexander, "Using Technology to Take Community Policing to the Next Level," *The Police Chief*, no. 78, July 2011, pp. 64–65. Copyright © 2011 by International Association of Chiefs of Police. All rights reserved. Reproduced by permission.

2. According to Alexander, what is the drawback for agencies in real-time sharing of information on social media?

3. What pros and cons must an agency consider in establishing a social media presence, in the author's opinion?

The Boca Raton, Florida, Police Services Department (BRPD) was one of the first law enforcement departments in the country to embrace social media. It happened in 2007, when this affluent oceanfront city fell into the national spotlight because of a double homicide of a mother and her daughter at an upscale mall. The department turned to one of the only widespread social networking sites at the time, Myspace, to post information and ask for anonymous leads in the case. This was considered a unique way for a law enforcement organization to investigate a crime and look for leads. In 2011, the BRPD is still on the cutting edge of social media. With Facebook, Twitter, YouTube, and blogs, the agency uses all means available via technology, including the introduction of Quick Response (QR) codes as one of the latest electronic tools.

Why use this technology? The reason is fairly simple. Boca Raton, whose population fluctuates from 89,000 in the summer to approximately 130,000 during the winter months, also has several large corporations within the city limits making the weekday, daytime population around 300,000. This fluctuating population is served by just fewer than 200 sworn officers and approximately 100 civilian employees. Using various social media platforms allows the department to communicate and inform residents, visitors, and those doing business in the city. It also allows those who live elsewhere part of the year with a way to follow the happenings in the city.

At the same time the department began using social media, it also hired a public relations firm. The reason was simple: BRPD employees view their department as a business and those that work, live, and visit the city as customers. So what did those customers think about the business serving them? To find out, the department set up a series of focus groups over four days with a total of 40 community members. The groups provided both positive and negative feedback and also helped to shape future branding plans and the department's social media strategy.

With the agency's assistance, the department developed the Visibility, Intelligence, Partnerships, Education, and Resources (VIPER) branding that has become synonymous with the BRPD throughout the region. The department and the public relations firm collaborated to create a logo along with a number of highly visible marketing campaigns aimed at crime prevention throughout the city.

Clearly Defined Goals

In addition to strong branding and a solidified view of its role in the community, the BRPD also has clearly defined goals regarding social media outreach. Effectively engaging the community is the number one priority of the department's social media and overarching communications strategies. Therefore, instead of merely pushing information out, the BRPD's social networking sites are designed to allow for open, two-way communication. This philosophy and the practice of communicating content immediately to the public allow for heightened levels of transparency—a characteristic that is valued by the city government in Boca Raton and by communities across the United States. Further, these new channels of communication allow BRPD employees to show their customers what the department is doing and highlight efforts that are routinely overlooked by traditional media outlets.

By using social media, the BRPD has been able to effectively market itself within its community, increasing awareness and establishing positive relationships. The reason is simple: The media is not what it used to be. Between the challenging economy and budget cuts, most media outlets have made drastic cutbacks that not only affect the way they cover the news but also what they cover. When it comes to getting information out to the public, law enforcement has always turned to the media. Now reporters find themselves having to decide what story to cover that day, no longer able to cover it all. This means many stories go unreported. The lack of coverage leaves citizens uninformed about crimes or arrests in their communities.

The BRPD uses several forms of social media, including Twitter, Facebook, YouTube, and its own website at http://www.ci.boca-raton.fl.us/police. Critics question the use of social media, saying it releases too much information without adequate filtering. However, at the BRPD, the same information that would normally be released to the public is posted on social media sites—no more, no less. The only difference is the information is closer to being available in real time. Unlike the traditional methods of emailing or faxing releases to local television stations and newspapers and waiting for broadcasts or publications, social media facilitates a real-time approach.

This system does have its drawbacks. The department generally does not have as much time to think about and massage the language that is being posted as quickly as possible on Facebook, for example, as it does when a traditional press release is drafted and released. Once the send button is pushed, the message is difficult to retract.

Yet in times of crisis, social media becomes a direct link between the police and the public. During natural disasters, social media can prove to be an incredibly valuable tool. Agencies can communicate information to the public more quickly through tweets and Facebook posts than they can through radio, television, and even online media. For example, during a hurricane, a public information officer (PIO) can constantly update citizens on evacuations, street closures, flooding, and storm conditions almost as they occur. The public, media officials, and anyone else following the law enforcement agency online will receive the updates simultaneously. The two-way nature of social media also provides an excellent mechanism for law enforcement to gather information from community members.

Obstacles Had to Be Overcome

Because social media provides a dynamic way to connect with a rich and diverse online community, it has yet to be fully embraced by many law enforcement administrators. Here are some of the obstacles that the BRPD has had to overcome.

1. It's fast, and we're not. We have to take our time.

The allure of social media, particularly Twitter, is speed and efficiency. The Miracle on the Hudson—the plane crash into the Hudson River in New York City after both engines were disabled but in which there were no fatalities—demonstrated how quickly an item can be reported via social media and then spread like wildfire.

How often does the public hear the police public information line about it being too premature to comment on an ongoing investigation? Police officials are not trying to stall for the sake of building drama; instead, they have to build an airtight case and cannot release information that will jeopardize their investigation. Often, police officers are working several different angles, including multiple interviews and the careful collection of evidence.

In this new media world order, no one has the patience for all of the facts to emerge. Law enforcement officials are now struggling with telling the story quickly and, at least as far as Twitter is concerned, in fewer than 140 characters.

2. We sometimes creep people out.

Consider this actual event: A tweeter that the Twitter handle for the BRPD, @bocapolice, decided to follow received this ominous message: "Boca Raton Police (@BocaPolice) is now following your tweets on Twitter." He said that he found this message disconcerting. Consider this comment from a different tweeter: "I was alerted that @bocachief was following me. I hope I wasn't speeding."

There is truth in humor. When law enforcement officers in uniform encounter ordinary citizens, it is not uncommon for one of these citizens to jokingly say, "I didn't do it!" Parents sometimes point to the officer and warn their misbehaving children that the officer will put the kids in jail if they do not behave appropriately. It is not surprising that firefighters do not receive these same types of reactions, and it is unlikely anyone will ever hear a parent saying, "Behave or that paramedic will stick you with a needle."

People generally still trust police officers but are naturally anxious about being social with law enforcement. Ordinary citizens often have their first and only interactions with officers during traffic stops. This does not seem to be the best time to ask a citizen to follow the department in the social media universe. Imagine this: "Please sign the citation, and be sure to follow us on Twitter." Not a great way to connect.

3. It's personal, and we are not.

There are a number of reasons why police officers seem to be impersonal at times. They are programmed to always be on alert for an imminent attack. Some Boca Raton residents are not willing subjects or witnesses and, frequently, they are not happy to see the police. Because cases are often built on solid legal standards, police officers can project a "just the facts, ma'am" image.

Law enforcement also sees the worst of the human condition, sometimes making it difficult for officers to relate to citizens in a meaningful way. If officers do amass friends and followers online, they are typically a select group of like-minded individuals.

Even in the subconscious, police officers often like to gather intelligence on who they are dealing with before they become comfortable with an individual. The insanely wide-

A Virtual Arsenal of Automated Information

Real-time information can greatly influence how officers work. Let's imagine an officer responding to a call for service using real-time information; he or she is now armed not only with a gun, but also with a virtual arsenal of automated information. The technology instantly makes available relevant data about the caller, the address, the type of call, and its association with community-identified problems. With this new "big picture" view, the call is no longer treated as just another service call, but rather as an event that is associated with the larger crime and disorder problems the police and community are attempting to address.

Barbara McDonald and Ron Huberman, Community Policing: The Past, Present, and Future, *2004.*

open world of social networking does not correspond well with that cynical frame of reference.

4. We are afraid of getting burned.

Police officers represent authority, have been given a lot of power, and are held to a higher standard. Right or wrong, they are easy targets of verbal attacks.

The by-product of using social media effectively is increased exposure. While transparency is currently in demand, it generally does not make police officers feel secure.

5. We cannot handle the volume.

The police PIO is often the sole person responsible for handling social media for the agency. Traditional PIO work is event-driven, involving organized communication primarily with the media. Social media is constant, ever changing, and involves multiple points of contact. The PIO now has to develop content, update multiple sites, and be responsive to many customers in this evolving form of communication.

The Benefits Outweigh the Costs

The benefits of social media outweigh the costs. There are ways to easily overcome these potential roadblocks, allowing law enforcement to leverage social media to take community policing to another level. Police administrators must consider the following when weighing the pros and cons of a social media presence.

- Does it make sense to ignore a huge audience of constituents?

- Does the agency want other people defining its message to this enormous audience?

The key is identifying what elements work for individual agencies, and then engaging the elements.

> "Effective community policing must respond to the needs of distinct neighborhoods and communities."

Community Policing Must Adapt to Different Communities' Needs

John Markovic

In the following viewpoint, John Markovic argues that for community policing to be successful, it must be responsive to the unique needs and characteristics of neighborhoods. He asserts that this approach, called situational policing, views communities as dynamic and promotes the police's role in helping neighborhoods reach a stage where residents, local organizations, and authorities are interdependent. This form of law enforcement, Markovic notes, is relatively new and unproven, but supports problem-solving that focuses on the distinct features of communities to strengthen them and to allow them to work in better cooperation with authorities. Markovic is a senior social science analyst at the Office of Community Oriented Policing Services at the US Department of Justice.

John Markovic, "Neighborhoods Matter: A Situational Policing Perspective," *Geography and Public Safety*, vol. 2, no. 2, December 2009, pp. 10–12. Reproduced by permission.

As you read, consider the following questions:

1. How must the police be prepared to support a situational policing approach, according to Markovic?

2. How does the author characterize a vulnerable neighborhood?

3. What does a neighborhood in a dependent stage lack, as explained by Markovic?

Effective community policing must respond to the needs of distinct neighborhoods and communities. In *Defining the "Community" in Community Policing*, Daniel W. Flynn comments on the challenges of community policing that larger police departments serving diverse populations face.

> [A typical jurisdiction] is composed of a collage of various areas or neighborhoods comprising assorted socio-economic groups, ethnic groups and groups of particular types of businesses or industries. Thus, for the purposes of community policing, it becomes necessary to subdivide the jurisdiction into several smaller communities to tailor problem-solving efforts to the communities' unique problems. Ideally, successes in each of the smaller communities will combine to create a synergistic effect resulting in jurisdiction-wide crime reductions, enhanced public safety and improved public satisfaction with the police.

Flynn's perspective suggests that collaborations between police and residents should be tailored to specific neighborhood needs and attentive to the dynamics of neighborhoods as they change over time. Police must consider both geographic and cultural aspects of neighborhoods, and respond to specific contextual and situational factors in a community that may inhibit or induce crime. These include protective factors, such as community organizations that promote prosocial values, and risk factors, such as tensions between different socioeconomic or ethnic groups within the neighborhood.

Situational Police Style by Neighborhood Type

Interdependence/collaboration with police

Style 1: Supporting and Recognizing

Strong Neighborhood

Style 4: Systems, Planning, and Response

Responsive Neighborhood

Low Crime and Disorder

Conflict

High Crime and Disorder

Style 2: Substituting and Selling

Vulnerable Neighborhood

Style 3: Securing, then Organizing

Anomic Neighborhood

Dependence on police

TAKEN FROM: John Markovic, "Neighborhoods Matter: A Situational Policing Perspective," *Geography and Public Safety*, vol. 2, no. 2, December 2009.

This article examines situational policing, a recent extension of the community policing concept that identifies individual types of neighborhoods, and considers how police can work across these differences to both strengthen neighborhoods and reduce crime. It also discusses the policy implications associated with identifying and policing distinct neighborhood types.

Situational Policing

The concept of situational policing was introduced by [researchers] James Nolan, Norman Conti, and Jack McDevitt in

2004. Building off an underlying conceptual model and with financial support from the Office of Community Oriented Policing Services, Nolan and colleagues' current work uses a comprehensive assessment, or process model, designed to help reduce crime and make neighborhoods safer. The process model does this by first identifying and understanding neighborhood types and then taking appropriate and necessary steps to develop strong neighborhoods.

Situational policing recognizes that communities are dynamic and developing entities. It supports the idea that police can help move communities through developmental stages, eventually leading to interdependent partnerships among residents, community and civic organizations, and the police. In some neighborhoods, police must stabilize the area before the residents can begin to organize. In other neighborhoods, police can rely on existing social capital and collective efficacy.

Beyond assessing a neighborhood's crime and disorder problems, situational policing calls for an assessment of underlying factors that contribute to a particular neighborhood's cohesiveness (or lack thereof). Thus, situational policing requires sophisticated analysis that extends beyond traditional crime analysis. To support a situational policing approach, police must be prepared to assess a neighborhood's capacity to organize itself and work with the police. In particular, this includes law enforcement's ability to assess a neighborhood's unique culture, key community stakeholders (e.g., clergy, local politicians, and business owners), demographics, and capacity for collective efficacy.

Neighborhood Types

Nolan and colleagues are developing analytic tools that police can use to tailor community policing strategies to each neighborhood type. To date, the researchers have developed a community questionnaire that they are administering to residents in Cleveland [,Ohio]; Morgantown, West Virginia; Pittsburgh,

[Pennsylvania]; and Wilmington, Delaware. The project plans to create a comprehensive guidebook that will introduce the concept of situational policing to law enforcement practitioners, document the skills needed to assess and respond to the needs of individual neighborhoods, and provide specific tools and strategies that will help agencies implement situational policing approaches.

Situational policing stresses that individual neighborhoods vary in their degree of readiness to engage in collective action and in their ability to work effectively with police. Nolan and colleagues posit four neighborhood types, which vary along two dimensions: (1) the level of crime/disorder in the neighborhood, and (2) the degree to which a neighborhood depends on the police or has established interdependence (i.e., is capable of collaborating with the police). Each neighborhood type requires a different police response. . . .

Strong neighborhoods. Strong neighborhoods have a high degree of interdependence and low levels of crime. Residents in strong neighborhoods show a willingness to partner with each other and readily engage with community and civic organizations, including the police, in achieving shared goals. Police provide support while recognizing the strengths and social capacities that exist within the neighborhood.

Vulnerable neighborhoods. Vulnerable neighborhoods experience low levels of crime and disorder and low levels of interdependence and collective efficacy. Without a clear sense of neighborhood or the capacity to act collectively, residents of these areas tend to rely on police to provide formal social control. Because residents do not have a shared sense of belonging, incivility or disorder (e.g., congregating youth or illegal parking) can escalate into more serious disturbances and crime problems if left unchecked. Policing in these neighborhoods involves focusing on disorder issues as a means of sustaining a neighborhood's status as a low-crime area.

Anomic neighborhoods. Anomic [lawless] neighborhoods are characterized by high rates of crime and disorder and low levels of collective efficacy. Residents of anomic neighborhoods depend on police for formal social control. Yet, because of high crime rates and historically tense relations with police, many residents of anomic neighborhoods consider the police ineffective. These residents are not sufficiently organized to help police fight neighborhood crime and disorder problems. Police responses in anomic neighborhoods may involve traditional reactive responses to crime. But officers should also support community organizing efforts and outreach as mechanisms to build trust and restore confidence in the police.

Responsive neighborhoods. Responsive neighborhoods have high levels of crime and disorder and high levels of collective efficacy. These neighborhoods tend to have high rates of poverty and other risk factors (such as single-parent households and underperforming schools). However, they have the advantage of strong "social capital" in the form of established churches, block clubs, and civic associations with high levels of community participation. Community stakeholders in these areas provide support for the neighborhood and effectively partner with the police. Police in responsive neighborhoods can capitalize on the social capital already in place and lend their expertise and resources to support public safety and crime reduction.

Neighborhood Stages

Nolan and colleagues suggest that neighborhoods can transition through or be trapped in various states of police dependency. A neighborhood may exhibit the characteristics of one of three development stages:

Dependence. Dependent neighborhoods need direction and leadership. Residents generally share the belief that police are competent, efficient, and able to provide the necessary services to promote public safety. However, these neighborhoods lack strong community leaders, so the police may need to actively work to establish leaders and strengthen community organizations to begin promoting higher levels of collective efficacy.

Conflict. Residents of conflicted neighborhoods have different expectations and assumptions about their roles in the neighborhood and the competency and effectiveness of local government entities, including the police. Neighborhoods in conflict include "up-and-coming neighborhoods" characterized by gentrification and displacement and declining neighborhoods with high rates of mortgage foreclosures and property abandonment.

Interdependence. Interdependence is the optimal state in which conflicts among members of a neighborhood are resolved. In interdependent neighborhoods, community members stand ready to work together with each other, the police, and other government entities toward common goals.

Policy and Practical Implications

Situational policing is grounded firmly on existing theories and has practical appeal. However, the situational community policing perspective is relatively new and untested. The perspective raises questions about whether situational policing can be generalized across and beyond urban neighborhoods. As this perspective emerges, a number of key policy and practical questions may arise, including:

- What level of collective identity needs to exist before a geographic area can develop a shared sense of neighborhood?

- Do certain geographic areas or neighborhoods have residents who prefer to remain independent?

- Do most residents in certain areas actually prefer dependent and reactive police services over active partnership?

- Are residents in neighborhoods that lack collective efficacy capable of or willing to change?

The situational policing perspective provides a theoretical framework for understanding neighborhood dynamics and their effect on crime. Rather than looking at crime patterns in isolation, it encourages analysts to assess the characteristics of a neighborhood that promote or inhibit collaboration with the police. Rather than imploring police to attack the "root causes" of crime, this perspective encourages a practical problem-solving approach that focuses on the unique characteristics of neighborhoods and how police can help make them stronger. As such, it provides a common frame of reference to help crime analysts, urban planners, government officials, and community groups to work more collaboratively. This promising theoretical perspective should be tested further by academics and analysts in applied settings.

> *"Feedback, or information flow, is essential for improving the relationships between the police and their communities."*

Improving Police-Community Relations Can Improve Community Policing

Katherine Freeman-Otte

In the following viewpoint, Katherine Freeman-Otte writes that police-community relations are key to implementing and improving community policing. She defines police-community-relations as ongoing communications between the people and police as the basis for law enforcement, the expansion of police responses beyond traditional constraints and procedures, police officers' compassion for solving human problems, and police-community relations as a continual process of mutual respect and feedback. According to Freeman-Otte, this differs from public relations, in which the main objective is to enhance the police's image. Based in Spokane, Washington, the author is a law student at Gonzaga University and a former intern at the city's Office of the Police Ombudsman.

As you read, consider the following questions:

1. In what ways can police agencies elicit feedback from the community, according to Freeman-Otte?

2. Why can public relations efforts be valueless and harmful to police agencies, in the author's opinion?

3. How, in Freeman-Otte's view, is police distrust of the community a block to police-community relations?

Community policing has become a viable operational model for many police agencies throughout the United States. It has many advantages over traditional policing.

Problems with community policing have been due not to the philosophy but to practitioners who usurp the title while still utilizing traditional policing strategies and who seek to implement changes without knowing what they are doing. Community-oriented policing moves from merely responding to reports of crime and/or requests for assistance to developing a proactive organization that works with its clients to determine what police services are needed and how to best provide these services. . . .

In order to gain intimate knowledge of the neighborhood, patrol officers must interact both formally and informally with the people of the community: residents, business operators, workers, even people who are just passing through the area.

Police-community relations seek to involve the citizen actively in determining what (and how) police services will be provided to the community and in establishing ongoing mechanisms for resolving problems of mutual interest to the community and the police—feedback and input. . . .

What "Community Relations" Means

- *Reviving the ideas of "the people's police."* This is the basic notion on which modern, urban police departments were founded. Needs for police service must be determined on the basis of ongoing communication between the people and the police.

- *A more reasoned basis for police work.* Police officers unusually operate with a repertoire of responses determined by penal codes, municipal ordinances, and demands of the often recurrent types of situations and emergencies with which they deal. The police-community relations concept encourages police to deal with complex problems in complex ways, going beyond traditional constraints and procedures where necessary.

- *A deeper, more comprehensive interest in human life.* To some, this phrase may sound sentimental, and to others, unnecessary, because many effective police officers now operate with humanity and compassion. Still, many police officers do not find it improper to adopt cynical attitudes toward human life. The police-community relations approach, by contrast, stresses that police are both entitled and required to take an interest in and help to resolve human problems.

- *An acceptance of the view that "relations" is a process, not a product.* It is vital, ongoing, and constantly changing. It requires mutual respect and mutual exchange and cannot be compartmentalized if it is to be effective. Feedback is a necessary ingredient of this process. The community and its groups must be encouraged to provide feedback to the people's police, and the police in turn must provide feedback to the community.

Public vs. Community Relations

Feedback, or information flow, is essential for improving the relationships between the police and their communities. In the past, police agencies ignored or set up shields to protect themselves from this feedback, not realizing the potential it

Contrasting Characteristics of Public and Community Relations in Police Departments

	Public Relations	Community Relations
Purposes	Attain/maintain good environment Inform public Enhance image Minimize obstacles Stimulate support	Develop police-community partnership Integrate community needs with police practices
Processes	Routinized functions Agency-oriented services One-way (outward) information flow Responsibility is compartmentalized	Flexible and adaptable functions Community-oriented services Two-way information flow Responsibility is dispersed throughout agency
Citizen Involvement	Consciously kept to a minimum	Actively sought and stimulated

TAKEN FROM: Ronald D. Hunter and Thomas Barker, *Police-Community Relations and the Administration of Justice*. Upper Saddle River, NJ: Prentice Hall, 2011.

had for system improvement or giving their "clients" the opportunity to act with and not merely be acted on.

Connection and communication

Police should do more than respond to incidents of crime by also helping neighborhoods solve problems that create crime and crime conditions. Good police-community relationships demand that feedback from the community is constantly solicited and evaluated by the police. Efforts to solicit feedback: community surveys, customer follow-ups, customer contacts, customer councils, focus groups, involvement in police activities, and complaint-tracking systems. The police must also solicit and involve themselves in providing feedback/input to other systems.

Public relations [PR] and community relations: a contrast

Police-community relations programs in the United States have been built on already existing public relations programs. Differences between police-community relations and police-public relations: different purposes, activities, reaction/interests. PR has no feedback or input.

Public relations activities are designed to create a favorable environment for agency operations by keeping the public informed of agency goals and operations and by enhancing the police image; the target is a citizen who passively accepts (and approves) what the police department is doing; there is no feedback or input. . . .

To what extent do primarily self-serving principles and practices affect a police agency's receptivity to community input? The answer to this question ultimately determines whether the agency is operating under a public relations or community relations philosophy. Public relations by itself can often prove valueless and even harmful to police agencies because its activities are agency oriented (and thus basically self-serving). Public relations officers are not agents of change and may gloss over or misrepresent crucial issues. On the other hand, every police agency must rely on public relations to some extent to help ensure its position in relation to other forces at work within the community. Public relations activities can play a valuable role in community relations programs provided they follow strict guidelines of honesty and integrity and make a goal such as image enhancement subordinate to providing better service. For crime prevention to be synonymous with police-community relations, crime-prevention efforts will need to meet police-community relations goals. Successful police-community relations must take into account exchange relationships among community groups located both

Public vs. Community Relations

	Public Relations	Community Relations
Purpose	Attain/Maintain good environment	Develop police-community partnership
	Inform public	Integrate community needs with police practices
	Enhance image	
	Minimize obstacles	
	Stimulate support	
Process	Routinized functions comprise activities	Flexible and adaptable functions comprise activities
	Agency-oriented services	Community-oriented services
	One-way (outward) information flow	Two-way information flow
	Responsibility compartmentalized	Responsibility dispersed throughout agency
Citizen Involvement	Consciously kept to a minimum	Actively sought and stimulated

Ronald D. Hunter and Thomas Barker,
Police-Community Relations
and the Administration of Justice, *2011.*

inside and outside the police organization. The police organization must be managed in a fair and competent manner that provides equal access and equitable treatment to all communities. Communication is the key not only to the police organization's success in police-community relations but also to its survival. . . .

When Community Relations Fail

When community relations efforts fail, at least one of the following blocks has contributed to that failure:

Community distrust of police

If the citizens do not trust the police, they will avoid police contact and they will not talk to them. Therefore, if distrust causes avoidance and failure to communicate, the implications for the police organization are very dramatic. Citizens will not report crime; they will not give statements to officers who are investigating crimes, and they will not testify in court. The result is inefficiency and an unsafe community.

Police distrust of community

If the police view the community or some geographical part of the community they have sworn to protect as dangerous and full of people who are hostile towards them, police will react in a negative way. They will not feel free to communicate with the community and will be guarded and cautious when they come in contact with those they are protecting. As a result, police officers will contribute to widening the gap between themselves and the rest of the community. Their belief system will be reinforced by negative community contacts. Eventually, police officers will become fearful and hostile toward the very people they are supposed to be protecting and serving.

Training

Training must develop interpersonal skills, such as active listening, de-escalation techniques and proactive problem-solving skills. The training must stress cultural diversity and the need for the police to become part of the community not apart from the community. The police must incorporate community policing into their training. The police officer of the twenty-first century will be someone capable of critical and independent thinking and who can work with other agencies and culturally diverse community members to solve community problems.

Organizational structure

Paramilitary organizations normally strengthen command authority; however, this structure has the opposite effect in police departments. Police superiors do not direct the activity of officers in any important sense, they are perceived as mere disciplinarians. Contrary to the army officer who is expected to lead his men into battle, the analogously ranked police official is someone who can only do a great deal to his subordinates and very little for them. For this reason, supervisory personnel are often viewed by the line personnel with distrust and even contempt. More importantly, paramilitary organizational structure not only blocks effective communication within the organization because of the superior-subordinate relationship, but the same working relationship is inevitably transferred to contacts between patrol officers and citizens.

> "A well-developed strategic plan can assist in knocking down barriers to the implementation of community policing."

Planning the Implementation of Community Policing

Michael J. Palmiotto

A former police officer, Michael J. Palmiotto is a criminal justice professor and undergraduate coordinator of the criminal justice program at Wichita State University in Kansas. In the following viewpoint, he claims that having a strategic plan smooths the transition from a traditional policing model to a community policing model. Palmiotto contends that planning puts organizational goals into focus, which enables the concentration of resources on priorities, provides a blueprint for processes and responsibilities, and encourages long-range thinking and better coordination of actions. Finally, he maintains that a strategic plan will help gain the support from police personnel and community members that is necessary for success.

As you read, consider the following questions:

1. According to Palmiotto, what does a strategic plan include?

2. What are the drawbacks to planning and acting simultaneously, in the author's view?

3. How does Palmiotto describe "bottom-up thinking," which he recommends for community-policing plans?

As Malcolm Sparrow (1982) remarked, those who accept the desirability of introducing community policing confront a host of difficult issues: What structural changes are necessary, if any? How do we get the people on the beat to behave differently? Can the people we have now be forced into the new mold, or do we need to recruit a new kind of person? What should we tell the public, and when? How fast can we bring about this change? Do we have enough external support?

Before community policing can be implemented to any degree in a police organization, a plan must be established to address such questions and many others. A plan often will depend upon the size of the police organization and the number of qualified personnel who are familiar with the planning process. Large police organizations may have a planning section with trained planners, whereas small ones may not have any trained planning personnel or planning unit. Depending on whether there are planning personnel, a police organization may have either a very detailed strategic plan or a "plan as you go" approach. A "plan as you go" approach may have goals, objectives, and a mission for implementing community policing, but goals and objectives are not detailed, and there may not be any consideration of potential problems, issues, or impediments to implementing community policing. A strategic plan includes mission, vision, and values statements, goals and objectives, analysis of community and department needs and resources, analysis of potential obstacles, action steps for accomplishing goals, time frames and sometimes personnel assignments for action steps, and mechanisms of monitoring and assessment.

Police departments that have the capabilities to develop a strategic plan are advised to do so. A well-developed strategic plan can assist in knocking down barriers to the implementation of community policing. Both police personnel and members of the community should be involved in the planning process. A well-thought-out strategic plan should make community policing easier to implement and increase chances of obtaining the support of police personnel and community members.

The transition from traditional policing to community policing is not easy, and this must be taken into consideration by the chief executive of the police organization. Patience and understanding are important in implementing community policing.

What Is Planning?

Planning has been defined as "setting objectives and deciding how to achieve them" (Tansik and Elliott 1981, 33), or, in more detail, as:

> A management function concerned with visualizing future situations, making estimates concerning them, identifying the issues, needs and potential points, analyzing and evaluating the alternative ways and means for reaching desired goals according to a certain schedule, estimating the necessary funds and resources to do the work, and initiating action in time to prepare what may be needed to cope with changing conditions and contingent events. (Mottley 1972, 127)

Planning entails decision making; it involves selecting a route that an organization will follow. There are various types of plans, ranging from the detailed to the broadly defined plan for getting organizational goals on track. Planning asks the basic questions, What to do? How to do it? When to do it? Who will do it? (Koontz et al. 1986, 35).

Plans to implement community policing vary a great deal in scope. Some are plans to set up a special community policing unit within a department that is free from responding to radio calls and is thus able to work on community problems full time. Others are plans to turn every officer in the department into a community policing officer. Some plans cover a specific neighborhood, others an entire city. The scope of the plan will generally depend upon the size of the agency, the number of police personnel who can be assigned to the plan, the ability of the police organization to accept innovation, the extent of changes required, and the expectations of the community concerning the police. But even agencies with ambitious plans tend to start out small and initiate community policing in a single neighborhood.

Why Plan

Planning brings an organization's present situation into line with its goals for the future and lets members of an organization know what these goals are so that they can more effectively accomplish the organization's mission. By focusing on organizational goals, it allows the organization to concentrate its resources on goal-oriented priorities. It provides a blueprint and a process for achieving goals and makes clear who is responsible for what. It allows administrators to anticipate problems and to think about how to sidestep them or lessen their impact. It encourages long-range thinking. It cuts down on haphazard actions and makes possible better coordination of action so that different actions do not undercut each other or cancel each other out. Finally, it increases the chances of obtaining the external and internal support necessary for the plan to succeed (Whisenand and Ferguson 1989, 157–159). A plan should be considered as a specified outline of the format to be executed. A plan follows the following points:

1. The need for the plan must be recognized. An apparent need must be verified by a more intensive investigation and analysis.

2. The objective must be stated, and the general method of operation (the manner in which the objective is to be attained) must be determined.

3. Data necessary in the development of the plan must be gathered and analyzed. Included will be answers to the questions of "what," "where," "when," "who," and "how."

4. The details of the plan must be developed: personnel and equipment must be provided and organized, procedures developed or applied, schedules drawn up, and assignments made.

5. Planning reports must be prepared.

6. Planners should participate in a staff capacity during implementation, if this is requested by persons carrying out the plan.

7. Plans must be reviewed, and modified if necessary, to accommodate changes in need and technology. (Fyfe et al. 1997)

Silverman (1995) has vividly described the chaos and confusion that result from insufficient planning:

1. We are not sure what the problem is. Definitions of the problem are vague or competing, and any given problem is intertwined with other messy problems.

2. We are not sure what is really happening. Information is incomplete, ambiguous, and unreliable, and people disagree on how to interpret the information that is available.

3. We are not sure what we want. We have multiple goals that are unclear or conflicting or both. Different people want different things, leading to political and emotional conflict.

4. We do not have the resources we need. Shortages of time, attention, or money make a difficult situation even more chaotic.

5. We are not sure who is supposed to do what. Roles are unclear, there is disagreement about who is responsible for what, and things keep shifting as players come and go.

6. We are not sure how to get what we want. Even if we agree on what we want, we are not sure what causes what.

7. We are not sure how to determine if we have succeeded. We are not sure what criteria to use to evaluate success. If we do know the criteria, we are not sure how to measure them. (37–45)

In making the transition to community policing, planning is particularly important because community policing involves new concepts and strategies that may be unfamiliar to many people and that may conflict with many established police practices and organizational structures (see Chapter 9).

How Much Planning Before Implementation?

A key question facing police agencies is how far ahead and how extensively they should plan a community-policing program before putting it into operation. The Bureau of Justice Assistance (1994b) outlined three possible approaches, along with their strengths and weaknesses:

Strategic Planning Must Be Done First

It is because community policing is a philosophy and not a program, tactic, or technique that departments must be willing to devote the time, energy, and resources to strategic planning to implement and institutionalize this new form of decentralized and personalized police service. It is a mistake to think that the major planning effort can come later, after an initial experimental phase.

Bonnie Bucqueroux and Robert Trojanowicz,
Community Policing: How to Get Started, *1998.*

1. Plan, then implement. This method entails developing a detailed long-range plan, with tasks and timelines, and assigning officers to execute the plan. This approach clearly delineates a set of strategies and actions that impart a sense of direction to implementation efforts; however, and even a very detailed plan will be unable to predict the obstacles that will arise. In the absence of experienced-based feedback, some part of the implementation process may be miscalculated. Planning can also be complicated by the size of the staff involved. Keeping the planning staff relatively small may prevent the process from becoming unwieldy; however, it may not adequately represent all levels of command, function, and experience within the organization, thus creating the risk that the plan will not be implemented. Planning can also become excessive and may stifle enthusiasm.

2. Plan and implement. In this approach, planning and action occur simultaneously. While the planning process

continues, the agency, to get started quickly, involves more personnel at the outset and permits further planning to benefit from feedback. However, the agency risks false starts, confusion, and major blunders unless effective, rapid, and regular communication takes place between planners and implementers.

3. Implement with little planning. The third option is for an agency with little preparation or knowledge of the nature of community policing to quickly launch into the action phase and then, on the basis of feedback, to retool the effort and begin the cycle again. This process is continuous, with each reevaluation cycle advancing the idea of community policing a bit further within the organization. This approach assumes that a limited knowledge of community policing may prevent agencies from initially planning in a meaningful way. Advocates note that the almost immediate action will catch officers' attention at all organizational levels and will harness the existing enthusiasm to help mobilize support. However, the constant shifts in goals and actions can be highly unsettling to the organization and the community it serves. (29–30)

According to the Bureau, none of these approaches is the "one right way." Police administrators will have to choose among them on the basis of agency priorities, resources, and support for change.

Who Plans?

All personnel in a police department should be involved in planning, but the expectations from personnel will vary. Kuykendall and Unsinger (1979) describe general planning responsibilities of each of the three levels of administration:

1. Top management is concerned with long-range considerations and general planning, and considerable time is

invested in planning activities. In large police departments, top management is placing increasingly greater
reliance on specialized planning and research units.

2. Middle managers participate in development of all
   ranges of plans in the agency, oversee the short- and
   intermediate-range plans, develop many of the details in
   long- and intermediate-range plans, and usually play a
   key role in making adjustments in the execution phases
   of plans.

3. Supervisors participate in the planning process by overseeing operational plans, and in many small police departments may perform the functions of middle managers as well; they also assist in developing the specifics or
   details for translation of plans into action. (105)

But as discussed in Chapter 9, community policing requires a more democratic management style, and this should
begin in the planning for the transition to community policing, Therefore, all community-policing plans should include
not only the three levels of management but also line, staff,
and civilian personnel. Bottom-up thinking should be employed rather than top-down thinking. Command staff should
have limited involvement in strategic planning. A police officer could be the leader of the committee, and it would not
be a bad idea for the chief not to be on the committee.

Community policing especially needs the understanding
and support of line personnel if it is to have an impact on
their community. The gap between "management cops" and
"street cops" can be closed if management shows a willingness
to make the street cop an important component of
community-policing planning, and this can make a big difference in the plan's success. A study sponsored by the National
Institute of Justice of neighborhood-oriented policing of eight
cities found that gaining police acceptance was a principal ob-
stacle to implementing community policing and that officers

who had limited or no knowledge about community policing or who felt that they had no voice in planning it did not support its implementation (Sadd and Grinc 1996, 7–11).

The participation of a cross-section of personnel—administrators, middle managers, supervisors, line and staff personnel, civilian personnel, and representatives from all department units and divisions—makes it possible to deal with and overcome resistance to community policing at an early stage— for example, claims that too much work will be required, that the plan will be used against employees at a later date, or that the plan limits officers' law enforcement powers. The more people who see that their input is solicited and incorporated, the more support the plan will have.

Planning for community policing should also involve the community. A strategic plan created without soliciting the co-operation of the community is doomed to failure. The community must buy in to the plan for it to be implemented successfully. When a community-policing strategic plan involves the community, the process includes bringing together a community as a whole to plan the policing philosophy and practices in a specific geographic location and developing community consensus and political momentum to ensure long-term support and commitment to change (National Center 1997, 8).

Active community and neighborhood members, along with persons who reflect the diversity of the community, should be made members of the strategic planning team. Community team members should represent the interest of homeowners, apartment dwellers, and business owners. Planning should also involve other governmental and service agencies who are involved in communities and neighborhoods.

Notes

Adams, R.E., W.M. Rohe and T.A. Arcury. 2002. Implementing Community-Oriented Policing: Organizational

Change and Street Officer Attitudes. *Crime and Delinquency* 48(3):399–430.

Bureau of Justice Assistance. 1994a. *Neighborhood-Oriented Policing in Rural Communities: A Program Planning Guide.* Washington, DC: U.S. Justice Department.

-----. 1994b *Understanding Community Policing: A Framework for Action.*Washington, DC: U.S. Justice Department.

Fyfe, J.J. et al. 1997. *Police Administration.* 5th ed. New York: McGraw-Hill.

Koontz, H. et al. 1986. *Essentials of Management.* New York: McGraw-Hill.

Kuykendall, J.L. and P.C. Unsinger. 1979. *Community Policing Administration.* Chicago: Nelson-Hall.

McKee, A.J. 2001. "The Community Policing Evaluation Survey: Reliability, Validity, and Structure." *American Journal of Criminal Justice* 25(2).

Meese, E., III. 1991, *Community Policing and the Police Officer. Perspectives on Policing.* Washington, DC: National Institute of Justice.

Mottley, C. 1972. "Strategy in planning." In *Planning, Programming, Budgeting: A Systems Approach to Management,* 2nd ed., ed. J.F. Lyden and E.S. Miller. Chicago: Markham.

National Center for State, Local and International Law Enforcement. 1997. *Strategic Planning and Implementation.* Glynco, GA: Federal Law Enforcement Training Center.

Rossi, P.H., M.W. Lipsey, and H.E. Freeman. 2004. *Evaluation: A Systematic Approach,* 7th ed., Thousand Oaks, CA: Sage Publications.

Roth, J. and J.F. Ryan. 2000. *The COPS Program After 4 Years—National Evaluation.* Washington, DC: National Institute of Justice.

Rush, G. 1992. "Community Policing: Overcoming the Obstacles." *Police Chief*, October, 50–55.

Sadd, S. and R.M. Grinc. 1996. *Implementation Challenges in Community Policing: Innovative Neighborhood-Oriented Policing in Eight Cities*. Washington, DC: National Institute of Justice.

Silverman, E. 1995. "Community Policing: The Implementation Gap." In *Issues in Community Policing*, ed. P.C. Kratcoski and D. Dukes. Cincinnati, OH: Anderson.

Sparrow, M. 1982. *Implementing Community Policing. Perspectives on Policing*. Washington, DC: National Institute of Justice.

Tansik, D.A. and J. Elliott. 1981. *Managing Police Organizations*. Belmont, CA: Duxbury.

Ward, K., S. Chibnall, and R. Harris. 2007. *Measuring Effectiveness: Planning and Managing Evaluations of Law*. Washington, DC: Office of Community Oriented Policing.

Whisenand, P.M. and F. Ferguson. 1989. *The Managing of Police Organizations*. Englewood Cliffs, NJ: Prentice-Hall.

Periodical and Internet Sources Bibliography

The following articles have been selected to supplement the diverse views presented in this chapter.

Akbar Bajwa	"Smart Policing: Police Learn to Use Digital Mapping to Tackle Crime," *Express Tribune* (Pakistan), August 18, 2013. http://tribune.com /pk.
Bryan Bender	"US Officials Seek Lessons in Bombing Catastrophe," *Boston Globe*, May 5, 2013.
Indraji Basu	"Social Media Elevates Community Policing," Digital Communities, August 6, 2012. www .digitalcommunities.com.
John DeRousse	"Using Community Policing to Manage Police Equipment," *Community Policing Dispatch*, April 2010.
Steven Dye	"Policing in Local Law Enforcement: A Commitment to Getting Out-of-the-Car," *Police Chief*, October 2009.
The Economist	"Don't Even Think About It," July 20, 2013.
Zach Friend	"Predictive Policing: Using Technology to Reduce Crime," *FBI Law Enforcement Bulletin*, April 2013.
William Harvey	"The End of Professional Policing?," *Police*, August 14, 2013.
George J. Kelling and Catherine M. Coles	"Keeping Americans Safe: Best Practices to Improve Community Policing and to Protect the Public," *Goldwater Institute Policy Report No. 242*, February 16, 2011. www.goldwaterinstitute .org.
Shoshana Walter	"Those Gosh-Darn Criminals Can Go to Heck," *New York Times*, October 2, 2011.

OPPOSING
VIEWPOINTS®
SERIES

CHAPTER 4

Do Stand Your Ground Laws Empower Citizens?

Chapter Preface

The debate surrounding Stand Your Ground (SYG) laws became overtly racialized after the 2012 shooting death of Trayvon Martin, an unarmed seventeen-year-old African American, by George Zimmerman, a twenty-eight-year-old Neighborhood Watch volunteer of white and Hispanic descent. For example, a 2013 national poll conducted by Quinnipiac University indicated that support and opposition of SYD among whites and blacks is, literally, inverted: white voters supported it by 57 percent to 37 percent and black voters opposed it by 57 percent to 37 percent—with 6 percent undecided in both groups. "With these kinds of numbers, it's unlikely the movement to repeal 'Stand Your Ground' will be successful in most of the country," concludes Peter A. Brown, assistant director of the Quinnipiac Polling Institute.

Opponents assert that SYG laws are systematically racist. "Promoted by the right-wing American Legislative Exchange Council, these so-called stand your ground or castle doctrine laws institute racist vigilantism," argues sociology professor Eduardo Bonilla-Silva in his book *Racism Without Racists: Color-Blind Racism and the Persistence of Racial Inequality in America*, adding, "and, as one would expect in a racialized society, these laws have not been applied in a racially neutral manner." To support his position, Bonilla-Silva cites a 2012 analysis of nationwide crime data by John Roman, a senior fellow at the Urban Institute's Justice Policy Center. Roman found that whites have a much higher likelihood of being justified in killing blacks in states with SYG than they are in states without it.

Proponents, however, counter that SYG laws are not racially biased. Commentators John Lott and Sherwin Lott insist that blacks living in poor, crime-ridden urban areas benefit the most from SYG. "It makes it easier for them to protect themselves when the police can't be there fast enough," they claim, adding, "rules that make self-defense more difficult would impact blacks the most." In Florida, Lott and Lott suggest, African Americans make up 16.6 percent of the population, but account for more than 30 percent of defendants that invoke SYG. "Black defendants who invoke this statute to justify their actions are acquitted 8 percent more frequently than whites who use that same defense," they add. In the following viewpoint, the authors debate the necessity and justification of SYG in self-defense.

"*The vague [Stand Your Ground] measure opened the door for a rise in vigilante shootings.*"

The New Vigilantes: Trayvon Martin and the "Shoot First" Lobby

Chris Kromm

In the following viewpoint, Chris Kromm claims that the shooting of unarmed Florida teen Trayvon Martin is an example of how Stand Your Ground (SYG) laws promote vigilantism. The shooter, neighborhood watch volunteer George Zimmerman, had pursued Martin despite instructions from the 911 operator, Kromm states, and was not initially arrested or charged after the incident. And since Florida passed its vague law in 2005, Kromm alleges that the state's rate of "justifiable homicides" has jumped. Pushed aggressively nationwide by the gun lobby, the legal concept endorses a "shoot-first mentality" based on suspicions and race, Kromm maintains. The author is executive director of the Institute for Southern Studies, a civil rights research and policy center.

Chris Kromm, "The New Vigilantes: Trayvon Martin and the 'Shoot First' Lobby," *Facing South*, March 2012. Copyright © 2012 by Facing South. All rights reserved. Reproduced by permission. Original article available at: www.southernstudies.org/2012/03/the-new-vigilantes-trayvon-martin-and-the-shoot-first-lobby.html.

As you read, consider the following questions:

1. What similarities do the 2012 Florida shooting and 2007 Texas shooting Kromm describes share?

2. What statistics does Kromm cite to support his argument that justifiable homicides increased after SYG was enacted in Florida?

3. How did Marion Hammer describe opponents of SYG laws in Florida, as cited by the author?

In 2007, 61-year old Joe Horn looked out the window of his Pasadena, Texas home and saw a pair of black men in his neighbors' yard, apparently involved in a burglary. Horn called 911, and, as journalist Liliana Segura would later report, became agitated, deciding he needed to stop the crime himself:

> "I've got a shotgun," Horn told the 911 dispatcher. "You want me to stop him?"

> The dispatcher tried to talk him down. "Nope, don't do that," he told Horn. "Ain't no property worth shooting somebody over, OK?"

> It was not OK with Horn. With the dispatcher still on the phone, he grabbed his gun, went outside, yelled, "Move, you're dead!"—and shot the two men in the back.

Both men—Colombian immigrants Diego Ortiz and Miguel de Jesus—were declared dead on the scene.

The details of the case differ somewhat from the February shooting of Trayvon Martin in Florida that's generated a national uproar; there's no evidence, for example, that 17-year old Martin was engaged in any criminal act.

But the two fatal shootings also share eerie similarities: Both involved black "suspects" being gunned down by armed, non-black residents taking the law into their own hands. In both cases, the 911 dispatchers tried to prevent a vigilante shooting.

And both cases ignited debate about state laws—pushed aggressively over the last decade by the nation's gun lobby—that allow people who aren't law enforcement officials to use deadly force on the mere suspicion that someone else is putting their life or property at risk, a decision easily infused with racial stereotypes.

The New Vigilantism

In 2005, Florida passed the first "Stand Your Ground" law in the country. It was an expansion on the Castle Doctrine, a legal concept now codified by over 20 states that declares individuals have the right to defend their person or homes with force.

"Stand Your Ground," which was signed by Gov. Jeb Bush, took the concept one step further. Even away from the home, the statute says, a person can "meet force with force, including deadly force if he or she reasonably believes it is necessary to do so to prevent death or great bodily harm to himself or herself or another or to prevent the commission of a forcible felony."

The law further "provides that person is justified in using deadly force under certain circumstances," and "provides immunity from criminal prosecution or civil action for using deadly force."

As many predicted, the vague measure opened the door for a rise in vigilante shootings: As the *Tampa Bay Times* reported in October 2010, "justifiable homicides" tripled after the law went into effect. By 2009, two deadly shootings a week were being excused as warranted under the new law.

Florida's rise in extra-legal deadly shootings reflects a national trend: As more states have enacted laws embracing the Castle Doctrine or variations of "Stand Your Ground," the number of "justifiable homicides" has also grown.

According to FBI crime statistics, in 2005 there were 196 cases nationally where a killing was deemed "justifiable." By

R.J. Matson, Cagle Cartoons.

2010, that number had grown to 278, leading critics to warn about a rising "shoot-first mentality" that was taking hold in states with the new laws.

The Shoot-First Lobby

Only 20 lawmakers voted against Florida's "Stand Your Ground" bill in 2005, but that's largely a testament to the power of the state's gun lobby.

The lead lobbyist pushing the bill was infamous National Rifle Association lobbyist Marion Hammer. Hammer earned noteriety in the 1980s, when she called those supporting a tweak to the state's conceal carry law a "modern-day Gestapo."

Republicans quickly distanced themselves from Hammer, saying she had "lost any effectiveness or credibility she might have" with such inflammatory rhetoric; another said she had the "lowest standard of integrity I have ever seen for a lobbyist" in Florida.

167

But that didn't stop Hammer: In 1996, she told *The New York Times* that the solution to the nation's gun debate was to "get rid of all liberals."

But that was tame compared to the demagoguery Hammer used to push SB 436. She labeled all opponents—which included the National District Attorneys Association, the Florida Prosecuting Attorneys Association, and police chiefs from cities including Miami and St. Petersburg—as "bleeding heart criminal coddlers" who wanted Florida residents to "turn around and run" instead of protecting their family and property.

Even though they couldn't point to a single case where a law-abiding gun owner had been prosecuted for legitimate self-defense, Hammer and the gun lobby even stoked fears that lack of the law would leave residents "on their own" in the supposed fight for survival after hurricanes.

Concerns that it may lead to tragedy like Trayvon Martin's shooting? "Emotional hysterics."

Florida Republicans not only passed "Stand Your Ground," they later successfully lobbied to install Hammer in the Florida Women's Hall of Fame.

The victory in Florida emboldened the NRA to push for more state laws to allow the use of deadly force. As of January 2012, 30 states had some version of the Castle Doctrine; 17 states, clustered in the South and West, have versions of the more aggressive "Stand Your Ground" law.

This year [in 2012], the NRA pledged to bring a version of the self-defense law to all 50 states.

Legal Killing?

Back in Florida, the authors of "Stand Your Ground" are now saying the law shouldn't apply in George Zimmerman's shooting of Trayvon Martin. Because the 911 tape clearly shows Zimmerman deciding to pursue Martin, that rules out the "justifiable" use of force. As McClatchy [newswire] reported:

"They got the goods on him. They need to prosecute who-ever shot the kid," said [Durell] Peaden, a Republican who sponsored the deadly force law in 2005. "He has no protection under my law."

But what if Martin's shooting hadn't caught national attention thanks to an explosion of celebrity tweets and other social media? As of this writing, local police still have yet to charge Zimmerman in the shooting, which they have claimed falls under the self-defense statute—a decision they made based on Zimmerman's increasingly untenable assertion that he was being attacked.

In Texas in 2007, Joe Horn also claimed that "he was afraid for his life" in justifying his fatal shooting. But like the Martin case, the 911 tapes are damning in showing that Horn's life clearly was never at risk—he, like Zimmerman, *pursued* the supposed burglars, even though they weren't even on his own property.

In the summer of 2008, Joe Horn was cleared of any wrongdoing. A grand jury failed to indict Horn, thanks largely to the Castle Doctrine law that came into effect in 2007.

Indeed, the 911 tapes show Horn knew about the law, and guessed that—even though his claim to self-defense was shaky at best—it would give him immunity to shoot. As Horn told the dispatcher, who was vainly trying to dissuade him from shooting:

I have a right to protect myself too, sir . . . And the laws have been changed in this country since September the first, and you know it and I know it.

As Stephanie Storey, the fiance of one of the men killed by Horn, would later say:

This man took the law into his own hands. He shot two individuals in the back after having been told over and over to stay inside. It was his choice to go outside and his choice to take two lives.

And, thanks to the laws of vigilante justice in Texas and beyond, it was all perfectly legal.

> "Law enforcement often fails. . . . But
> the proactive aspects of policing, in-
> cluding confronting individuals who
> seem to be 'up to no good,' should be
> left to the professionals."

Standing Your Ground and Vigilantism

Robert VerBruggen

The neighborhood watch shooting of unarmed seventeen-year-old Trayvon Martin in 2012 ignited controversy surrounding Stand Your Ground (SYG) laws and vigilantism. In the following viewpoint, Robert VerBruggen agrees that the shooter, George Zimmerman, acted as a vigilante in pursuing Martin but insists that the duty to retreat should not be reinstated. VerBruggen persists that SYG protects innocent people under serious threat in the absence of the police. In other cases, however, the author argues, law enforcement should be left to the authorities. VerBruggen is an associate editor of the conservative magazine the National Review.

As you read, consider the following questions:

1. What commitment does armed self-defense require, as stated by VerBruggen?

Robert VerBruggen, "Standing Your Ground and Vigilantism," *National Review* online, March 2012. Copyright © 2012 by The National Review. All rights reserved. Reproduced by permission.

2. In VerBruggen's opinion, what makes Zimmerman a
   "classic cop wannabe"?

3. What solution does the author offer to vigilantism?

Florida has some of the strongest laws pertaining to armed
self-defense in the United States. Not only did the state begin the trend of "shall issue" concealed-carry laws in the late
1980s, but it more recently enacted a "Stand Your Ground"
statute, meaning that when a person faces a threat of death or
great bodily harm in a public place, he has no duty to retreat
from his attacker before using lethal force in self-defense.

However, a commitment to armed self-defense requires a
second commitment: to the principle that those who bear
arms must act responsibly. It is still not clear whether Florida
"neighborhood watch" vigilante George Zimmerman broke
the law when he chased down and killed 17-year-old Trayvon
Martin. And that's a problem, because Zimmerman acted in-
appropriately in the moments leading up to the shooting, and
Martin would still be alive if Zimmerman had behaved as he
should have. Supporters of pro-self-defense policies should
roundly condemn Zimmerman's actions, and Florida should
change its laws to prevent this incident from repeating itself.

The 28-year-old Zimmerman is a classic cop wannabe:
Loving the thought of himself as a police officer, and witness-
ing a spate of break-ins in his neighborhood, he decided to
patrol the streets in his SUV—carrying a gun (as he was li-
censed to do) and calling the cops 46 times over the course of
a decade to report "suspicious" activity. On the night of February 26, a black teenager happened to catch Zimmerman's
eagle eye.

At the outset of his call to the police, Zimmerman reports
that Martin "looks like he's up to no good, or he's on drugs,
or something—it's raining, and he's just walking around, looking about." Martin looks around at the houses, then starts

staring back at Zimmerman, and finally walks toward Zimmerman with his "hands on his waistband" to "check me out."

A car door opens, and Zimmerman says, "These a******s always get away." Zimmerman gives the operator directions to the scene—presumably while he starts to follow Martin, because Martin runs. As Zimmerman can be heard huffing and puffing, the operator asks if he's giving chase, and Zimmerman replies in the affirmative. "Okay, we don't need you to do that," the operator says. Zimmerman says "Okay," but keeps running anyhow.

What happened when Zimmerman caught up with Martin isn't entirely clear. Zimmerman told police that Martin jumped him from behind. Martin's girlfriend, who was on the phone with him while he was running, says that Martin asked "Why are you following me?"; Zimmerman replied "What are you doing here?"; and then a scuffle ensued. We do know that there was some sort of wrestling match, and that Martin landed some blows—Zimmerman was found with a bloody nose, grass stains on his shirt, and a wound on the back of his head. Toward the end of the fight a man was heard yelling, "Help! Help!" Zimmerman fired a single shot, and the screaming stopped.

Zimmerman's full account of what happened is not yet public, the neighbors didn't see very much, and while the yelling of "Help!" is captured on a 9-1-1 tape, there has not yet been an audio analysis proving whether it was from Zimmerman or Martin. The confrontation could have unfolded in any of a million different ways.

But regardless of what happened during the fight, Zimmerman's actions went well beyond defending himself and others from physical threats, and into the territory of vigilantism—and they should be illegal. Zimmerman sought out this confrontation, and as a result a young man is dead—a young man who was unarmed, who was not carrying drugs, and who very well may have done nothing more than defend himself against a stranger who followed him on the street. Trayvon Martin visited his father, walked to 7-Eleven to buy some Skittles during the halftime of the NBA All-Star game, and for that wound up dead at the hands of the "neighborhood watch."

Contrary to what many liberal pundits have written, Florida should not reimpose a "duty to retreat"—the policy that prevailed before Stand Your Ground—on innocent people who face violent attackers. But it is true that the Stand Your Ground statute protects people who don't merely stand their ground—it protects anyone who can reasonably claim he faced a serious threat, so long as he was "not engaged in unlawful activity" when the threat occurred.

Therefore, to arrest Zimmerman, the police would need evidence that he was doing something illegal when Martin attacked him, or that he didn't reasonably believe he faced a serious threat. Since we don't know whether Zimmerman threw the first punch when he caught up to Martin, and we don't know what Martin was doing when Zimmerman fired, this isn't possible.

The solution is to make Zimmerman's activity unlawful. It should be a crime to chase down a fellow citizen who runs away, except in certain situations (e.g. when a store owner pursues a shoplifter, as opposed to a man's running after a teenager with no provocation whatsoever). One might imagine this was already a crime—such as assault—but Florida police officials have said it is not.

Law enforcement often fails—that's why people need the tools to defend themselves, and the laws to protect them when they do so. But the proactive aspects of policing, including confronting individuals who seem to be "up to no good," should be left to the professionals. If Trayvon Martin had been approached by an officer who identified himself as such, rather than a strange man who jumped out of an SUV and chased him, he would almost certainly be alive today.

> "The [Stand Your Ground] law seems likely to encourage paranoiacs to misread and escalate anodyne situations."

Stand Your Ground Laws Put Safety at Risk

Justin Peters

In 2012, unarmed teenager Trayvon Martin was fatally shot by neighborhood watch volunteer George Zimmerman, who had confronted him. The shooting brought Stand Your Ground (SYG) laws under scrutiny and ignited debate on them. In the following viewpoint, Justin Peters contends that the laws—in affirming a person's right not to retreat under deadly attack and meet force with force—permit recklessness and aggression. First, he points out that no standard exists to define a life-threatening situation, and so the laws encourage the escalation of violence. Moreover, Peters contends, SYG makes the right to meet force with force appear to be an obligation. SYG promotes confrontation and allows vigilantes to avoid arrest and trial for violent offenses, he maintains. Peters is the crime correspondent for Slate, *an online magazine.*

As you read, consider the following questions:

1. When is SYG generally invoked, according to the author?

2. In the author's view, what is the difference between self-defense and SYG?

3. What anecdote does Peters offer to illustrate his position that SYG makes meeting force with force an obligation, not a right?

It's been just over a year since Sanford, Fla., neighborhood watch volunteer George Zimmerman shot and killed teenager Trayvon Martin [in February 2012], and the case remains as divisive and confounding as ever. Zimmerman claimed that he only fired after Martin initiated a physical confrontation. Early on, he avoided arrest thanks to Florida's "stand your ground" law, which requires police to show probable cause that a suspect used unlawful force. Here's the relevant part of Florida's statute:

> A person who is not engaged in an unlawful activity and who is attacked in any other place where he or she has a right to be *has no duty to retreat and has the right to stand his or her ground and meet force with force*, including deadly force if he or she reasonably believes it is necessary to do so to prevent death or great bodily harm to himself or herself or another or to prevent the commission of a forcible felony. (Emphasis is ours.)

Stand your ground didn't protect Zimmerman forever: He was ultimately arrested and charged with second-degree murder after a special prosecutor was appointed to oversee the case. Zimmerman's defense team has also indicated recently that it's unlikely he'll rely on a stand-your-ground defense at trial [Zimmerman was acquitted of all charges in July 2013]. Even so, the controversial law has continued to be a lightning rod, leading Florida Gov. Rick Scott to convene a bipartisan, multi-racial task force to study the legislation.

Last week [in February 2013], the task force issued its final report, which essentially concluded that stand your ground was fine as is. The report made several minor recommendations, some of which seemed like specific responses to the Martin case—that the legislature should clarify that neighborhood watch participants are not actually supposed to confront potential suspects, for example—but ultimately found that "all persons who are conducting themselves in a lawful manner have a fundamental right to stand their ground and defend themselves from attack with proportionate force in every place they have a lawful right to be."

There is a lot of common-sense support for the notion that a person shouldn't be found guilty of a crime if they act in self-defense. Stand your ground, though, is generally invoked in the early stages of a case, either in the hope that the cops won't make an arrest or that a judge won't let it go to trial.

Self-Defense vs. Stand Your Ground

People pleading self-defense generally must show that they made every possible effort to avoid violence. That includes retreating, except in the case where they're in their home—an old common-law principle known as the "castle doctrine." Stand your ground maintains that the world is your castle and that, if you're feeling threatened, you are under no obligation to retreat before fighting back.

The main conceptual difference between self-defense and stand your ground is that the former presumes a lawful society while the latter imagines a society under siege. I've stood in line at [Orlando, Florida's] Walt Disney World, and so I get why Floridians might think that anarchy rules their streets. But regardless, stand your ground is an odd and dangerous law, primarily because it is so vague. There's no absolute standard for determining that you are in danger of death or great bodily harm, and the law seems likely to encourage paranoiacs to misread and escalate anodyne [harmless] situations. This is the reason why we rely on paid police officers to

A Broad License to Use Deadly Force

Under prior Florida law, courts focused on whether a defendant could have avoided the confrontation. But now, whether deadly force was justified hinges on what the person "reasonably believe[d]." As a result, Florida residents have broad license to use deadly force in public. If a person is in a place where they have a right to be, is not acting illegally, and has not provoked violence, they can shoot without fear of the consequences so long as they "reasonably believe" they are threatened. Under a final provision, a person who claims their use of force was justified is immune from criminal prosecution and cannot be convicted unless prosecutors prove, beyond a reasonable doubt, that the defendant's fears were unreasonable.

Devonya N. Havis, Pursuing Trayvon Martin:
Historical Contexts and Contemporary Manifestations
of Racial Dynamics, *2013.*

defend us, rather than arming a bunch of jittery citizens and telling them to use their best judgment.

Moreover, I think the law encourages people to conflate the *right* to meet force with force with the *obligation* to meet force with force. If you're riding a city bus and a drunk guy tries to push past the bus driver without paying his fare, then, under stand your ground, you'd perhaps be technically justified in assaulting the guy. You had a right to be there. The drunk guy was using force. I'll take my key to the city, please!

Actual SYG Cases

Sure, this seems outlandish—until you read about some of the actual situations where stand your ground has been invoked.

Take the case of Michael Dunn, a white man who fired a pistol into an SUV filled with black teenagers in a Jacksonville parking lot, killing 17-year-old Jordan Davis. Though the confrontation began when Dunn asked Davis and company to turn down their music, Dunn claimed that he only fired after the car's occupants menaced him with a shotgun. Police have found no evidence that the occupants were armed. Dunn is expected to invoke stand your ground. [His trial was set to begin on February 3, 2014.]

What the Dunn case shows is that stand your ground can give people tacit permission to be more reckless and confrontational than they otherwise might. It's strange that some Florida lawmakers don't see this as a problem. Over the past few months, according to the *Orlando Sentinel*, Florida state legislators have introduced several bills designed to amend the law. Some of those bills aim to dial the law back; some don't. The latest, introduced this week [mid-March 2013] by Republican Neil Combee, would extend stand your ground protections to people who fire warning shots or brandish weapons in the hope of scaring away potential attackers.

I don't buy the argument that the world will be safer when people are allowed to pop off a round whenever they spot trouble in their rear-view mirrors. And I disagree with the idea that law-abiding citizens shouldn't ever have to retreat in the face of danger. The real world is not a *Death Wish* movie [about a vengeful vigilante]. It does not need more hyper-aggressive vigilantes who see it as their responsibility to take back the streets. George Zimmerman felt threatened by a stranger, so he shot and killed Trayvon Martin, who was armed with a can of tea and a bag of Skittles. A little more than a year later, I'm standing my ground: There should not be a law that allows someone who behaved like Zimmerman to avoid standing trial for his actions.

"The efforts to . . . repeal Stand Your
Ground and Castle Doctrine laws are
misguided."

Storming the Castle Doctrine

William J. Watkins Jr.

*After the 2012 shooting of unarmed Florida teen Trayvon Mar-
tin by neighborhood watch volunteer George Zimmerman, demands were raised for the repeal of Stand Your Ground (SYG)
laws. In the following viewpoint, William J. Watkins Jr. opposes
their repeal. According to him, self-defense or unjustified homicide is applicable in Martin's shooting, not SYG. Furthermore, he
argues, today's populations are in closer proximity to danger and
in more need of self-defense laws, Watkins adds. Repealing SYG,
he argues, would erode the legal security citizens require when
confronted with violence, whether in their homes or other places
lawful for them to be in. Watkins is the author of* Judicial Mon-
archs: The Case for Restoring Popular Sovereignty in the
United States.

As you read, consider the following questions:

1. What does the Castle Doctrine recognize about retreat,
   as stated by the author?

2. As claimed by Watkins, how do the True Man and Castle Doctrines circumscribe civil litigation?

3. What do opponents of SYG laws ignore about home invasions, in the opinion of the author?

Americans have been captivated by the February incident in Sanford, Florida, that resulted in the death of Trayvon Martin and the eventual arrest and charging of George Zimmerman. If the case could be resolved today, Trayvon Martin's family would still be without a son, George Zimmerman—even if exonerated—will never live a normal life, Sanford Police Chief Billy Lee's career is tarnished, and Al Sharpton's ego is even more bloated after succeeding in drawing worldwide attention to a local homicide investigation.

Agitators are using the Martin shooting to push for the repeal of state Stand Your Ground and Castle Doctrine laws, "When Rosa Parks was arrested, if we had focused on the bus driver and not on the states' rights law, we would have missed the point," lectured Jesse Jackson, "We must not just settle for Zimmerman, we must repeal the Stand Your Ground law." New York City Mayor Michael Bloomberg describes Stand Your Ground statutes as "shoot first laws ... [that] have undermined the integrity of the justice system and done serious harm to public safety." He is leading a national campaign to repeal the 25 state laws that permit the use of deadly force if the person being attacked is in a place where he has a lawful right to be and he reasonably believes such force is necessary to prevent death or serious bodily injury.

The efforts to distort and repeal Stand Your Ground and Castle Doctrine laws are misguided. The current campaign is actually an attempt to turn back the clock on a sensible development in American common and statutory law. In England during the Middle Ages, because the king claimed a monopoly on the use of force within his kingdom, homicide could be justified only if the perpetrator was executing the king's writ or when custom permitted (e.g., the taking of an outlaw without a warrant). In all other cases, including self-defense, conviction was required so long as the prosecution could prove that the defendant took a life. The defendant could apply for a pardon after conviction, but he had no legal defense. Later, the chancellor issued pardons in cases of self-defense as a matter of course, but the wait for a pardon was hardly a comfortable situation for the convicted felon who, say, had used deadly force to fight off a highwayman attacking his home or family.

As English law continued to develop it recognized a right of self-defense, but this was circumscribed by the duty to retreat. If a man was in the forest cutting wood (for his cottage) and got into a fight with a knife-wielding neighbor, the woodcutter had a duty to run away before using his ax to repel the neighbor. The woodcutter had to ensure that no reasonable means of escape existed before he struck the armed enemy with the ax. The law acknowledged one exception to this general duty to retreat; the Castle Doctrine. If an aggressor entered the woodcutter's home, the woodcutter possessed the right to use deadly force to defend against an attack without having to "retreat to the wall."

The Castle Doctrine recognizes that, when in the home, one has, in essence, retreated as far as possible. Requiring further retreat, such as fleeing from the kitchen area where the hypothetical bandit entered to the sleeping quarters, makes little sense. The Castle Doctrine also affirms that the home should be a sanctuary. A man's home is his castle, as the adage goes, and requiring retreat degrades the sanctity of the home and encourages felonious conduct.

In America, state and federal common law, for the most part, has rejected the duty of retreat found in English law. The "True Man Doctrine" became the rule in a number of American jurisdictions, although some states still adhere to the duty to retreat. Under the True Man Doctrine, a person without fault does not have to retreat from an actual or threatened attack if he is in a place where he has a right to be and he has a reasonable fear of death or serious bodily injury.

A seminal case explaining the True Man Doctrine is *Beard v. United States* (1895). Beard was a farmer whose life had been threatened by one Will Jones. Jones and his brothers claimed that a cow in Beard's possession rightly belonged to them. They armed themselves and went to Beard's property. Beard ejected them from the property, forbade them to come back, and explained that he would let them have the cow only if a court of law recognized their claim. Jones informed townspeople that he would kill Beard to get the cow and returned to the property armed with a pistol. Beard, returning from town (where he had learned about Jones' threats), was armed with a shotgun and saw Jones and his brothers arguing with Beard's wife over the cow. Beard approached the group and directed Jones to leave the premises. Jones refused to leave. He then marched toward Beard and reached into his pocket where a pistol was secreted. Beard used the butt of the shotgun to crack Jones' skull. Jones later died from this injury.

Beard was indicted for manslaughter and tried. During the jury charge, the judge instructed that Beard had a duty to retreat from Jones unless the attack occurred in Beard's home. Based on this instruction, the jury found Beard guilty, and he was sentenced to eight years in prison. On appeal, the Supreme Court reversed. In finding fault with the charge, the Court noted that "the accused was [not] under any greater obligation when on his own premises, near his dwelling house, to retreat or run away from his assailant, than he would have been if attacked within his dwelling house." Observing that the English duty to retreat had been modified in most American jurisdictions, the Court averred that "the tendency of the American mind seems to be very strongly against the enforcement of any rule which requires a person to flee when assailed, to avoid chastisement, or even to save a human life." Because of the error in the jury charge, the Supreme Court overturned Beard's conviction.

Twenty-six years later, the Court again rejected the duty to retreat in *Brown v. United States*(1921). Writing for the majority, Justice Oliver Wendell Holmes described the duty to retreat as inconsistent with human nature. An internal debate on whether retreat would lead to escape is not required when a man is faced with a potentially life-threatening circumstance. "Detached reflection," Holmes wrote, "cannot be demanded in the presence of an uplifted knife." If a man reasonably believes his life is in danger, "he may stand his ground" and kill the attacker if necessary.

Twenty-five states have enacted laws to clarify and solidify the True Man and Castle Doctrines. Legislators believed that statutory action was necessary for a variety of reasons. For instance, in modern society an automobile is practically an extension of the person. Hence, many states have extended the Castle Doctrine to an occupied vehicle. If a carjacker seeks to gain entry to your vehicle, there is no duty to retreat, and deadly force may be used to halt the attack.

Many of the statutes also circumscribe civil litigation if a person lawfully uses force in self-defense against an aggressor. These provisions appreciate the litigiousness of modern America. If a criminal court finds that a person acted reasonably in self-defense and thus the homicide was justified, the estate of the attacker should not be able to bring a civil case and hope to extort money from the person defending himself or his home. If the estate or another individual does bring suit, many of the laws contain fee-shifting provisions so the civil defendant may recover costs and attorneys' fees incurred in defending the claim.

Legislators also understand that courts can be fickle institutions. Just as courts have "discovered" rights to homosexual marriage in state constitutions, it would not be surprising for modern jurists to discover that Justice Holmes had it wrong and that the common law imposes a duty to retreat even if the victim has a reasonable fear of death or bodily injury. Statutes on the books were needed to protect the people from backsliding judges with little or no accountability to the electorate.

Opponents of the Stand Your Ground and Castle Doctrine statutes portray these laws as relics of Southern honor codes or Wild West vigilante justice. They paint the supporters of the laws as gun-toting rednecks (or maybe "white Hispanics") looking for a fight—especially with minorities. Thanks to these statutes, white trash has been given a green light to shoot first and ask questions later.

It's interesting that the recent Stand Your Ground and Castle Doctrine laws have little or no relevance to the highly publicized deaths that the usual suspects are exploiting to demand repeal. In the Martin shooting, Stand Your Ground does not apply, whether one believes Zimmerman's version or that of Martin's partisans.

If we believe Zimmerman, he shadowed Martin, eventually caught up with him, started to leave the area, was knocked to the ground, and had his head slammed into the concrete multiple times. He says he shot Martin because he feared for his life. Taking this as the truth, the duty to retreat is irrelevant because Zimmerman had his back to the wall (i.e., the ground) and had to shoot to save himself.

If we believe Martin's allies, then Zimmerman was the aggressor the entire time and shot Martin in cold blood. As the aggressor, Zimmerman cannot take advantage of Stand Your Ground and clearly committed an unjustified homicide.

Similarly, opponents of Wisconsin's Castle Doctrine statute say that it permitted Adam Kind to "execute" Bo Morrison. On March 3, Morrison was attending a drinking party next door to Kind's home in the small village of Slinger in Washington County. Kind confronted some of the partiers about noise and then called police. The police came, but the drunken

The Law Should Protect the Threatened

The duty to retreat puts the person at great risk, and it's a Monday morning quarterback situation. We can all sit and analyze for hours what someone could have done. But in fact, a victim of a violent attack has seconds to decide if they want to live or they want to die or they want to be a victim of violence, such as rape or a beating. And I think in those circumstances, we need to give that law-abiding citizen the benefit of the doubt and stand beside them and say if you can stop a violent act from occurring that's going to victimize you and your family, that we're going to stand with you.

Dennis Baxley, interviewed by Neal Conan,
Talk of the Nation, *NPR, March 26, 2012.*

juveniles barricaded themselves in a garage and refused to surrender. Once the police relocated down the street, Morrison and some of the others made a run for it. Morrison, who was out on bail for a list of charges, including battery and resisting or obstructing an officer, and whose blood alcohol level was twice the legal limit, entered the three-season porch of Kinds home and hid. Kind heard noise, feared for the safety of his wife and children, retrieved a pistol, and went to investigate. He encountered Morrison, who made a move toward him. Kind fired one round and killed the 20-year-old black male.

Washington County District Attorney Mark Bensen declined to press charges. Under the state's recently enacted statute, the prosecutor concluded that Kind was entitled to a statutory presumption that force was necessary to protect himself and his family. Even without this statutory presumption, the prosecution found that there was no common-law duty to retreat because Kind had actually walked past Morrison before he discovered him. To retreat effectively, Kind would have had to run from the porch to the yard, leaving Morrison inside with Kind's wife and children. Wisconsin's common law imposes no duty to abandon one's loved ones in such a situation. Consequently, even without the Castle Doctrine statute, the prosecutor determined that a case could not go forward.

Opponents of the Stand Your Ground and Castle Doctrine laws are wrong to argue that "true man" principles are relics of the 19th century. At the beginning of the 20th century, over 70 percent of the population lived in rural areas. Today only 16 percent of Americans live in a rural environment. If 19th-century Americans could stand their ground when an enemy living around the bend in the creek attacked, how much more the necessity today when the enemy lives on top of you in an apartment building? Communal dwelling means a greater proximity to danger and a greater need for laws permitting self-defense. Thus, the Stand Your Ground and Castle Doctrine statutes are more suited for modern circumstances than for 19th-century life.

The Sharptons and Jacksons also ignore that most home invasions generally take place in low-income urban areas that are disproportionately inhabited by minorities. It is not a stretch to assume that police response times might be much longer in these neighborhoods than in privileged areas of the community. Hence, the laws under assault actually offer more protection to the law-abiding minority folks whom the "civil rights" establishment claims it is defending.

The families of Martin and Morrison understandably grieve for lost loved ones. But the repeal of the Stand Your Ground and Castle Doctrine laws would not resurrect these young men or make similar incidents less likely.

Repeal would place the right to protect our persons and property on dubious ground. While crime rates have fallen in recent years, we are a far cry from mid-20th-century America, when citizens could leave front doors unlocked at night and permit children to play outside without supervision. Our precarious urbanized existence requires some legal security for citizens who use force when confronted with a home invader or who reasonably fear for their safety in places where they have a lawful right to be.

Surely the "tendency of the American mind" described in *Beard* has not been so warped that a general duty of retreat will replace Stand Your Ground and Castle Doctrine laws. If so, this will mark a further decay in our society. Like the medieval English woodcutter facing a robber in the forest, we will be forced to flee from aggressors until all avenues of escape are blocked. And if we do use deadly force to save ourselves or our families, we can only hope there arises an American chancellor to issue a pardon.

"One should seek all avenues to avoid any seriously escalated confrontation and only use deadly force if absolutely necessary."

The Use of Deadly Force Allowed in Stand Your Ground Laws Should Be a Last Resort

Joshua K. Roberts

The 2012 shooting of seventeen-year-old Trayvon Martin by neighborhood watch member George Zimmerman in Florida brought attention to Stand Your Ground (SYG) laws and the use of deadly force in self-defense. In the following viewpoint, Joshua K. Roberts reasons that SYG can be justified in certain circumstances but that deadly force must be the absolutely last course of action. He insists that it cannot be used to defend one's property or if a chance to retreat can be observed. Furthermore, the author cautions that SYG is not universal, as states with the laws interpret them differently and on a case-by-case basis. Based in Springfield, Missouri, Roberts is a partner with the law firm of Hazelrigg, Roberts & Easley P.C.

As you read, consider the following questions:

1. When does an intentional killing not constitute murder, as stated by Roberts?

2. According to the author, how is deadly force generally defined?

3. How does Roberts illustrate the distinction between defending property and defending life in the use of deadly force?

He circled his car around in the mist as he barked into his cell phone to the police dispatcher, telling her of the suspicious character he had seen walking behind the townhomes in his gated community. Ignoring the dispatcher's instruction not to follow the man and to wait for the police, the head of the neighborhood watch got out of his car and pursued the suspicious character. A confrontation ensued. Cries for help were heard by neighbors. And when the dust settled, George Zimmerman had a broken nose and was bleeding from the back of his head, while Trayvon Martin lay dead from a single gunshot wound to the chest. The legal battle that ensued brought the age-old question of the use of deadly force in self-defense back into the public eye.

Most civilized societies place a high value on human life. Rules and codes of conduct have been in place since the dawn of time to protect the sanctity of life and to guard against the unwarranted taking of human life. Almost all societies both present and in antiquity have considered the unjustified taking of human life a most serious crime worthy of the harshest of punishment. The first known prohibition against murder was handed down over 6,000 years ago to Moses, by way of the Ten Commandments, as recorded in the Bible in Exodus 20:13 and Deuteronomy 5:17. Today, all fifty states have statutes that prohibit murder.

The Concept of Murder

Therefore, any analysis of the use of deadly force in self-defense has to necessarily start with an examination of the concept of murder. Murder is the unlawful killing, with malice aforethought, of another human. Put another way, murder is the (1) intentional and (2) unjustified killing of another human being. Note that both elements are required for the act to be considered murder. Not all intentional killings constitute murder. A police officer gunning down a violent assailant in the line of duty, the killing of enemy soldiers during war or the lethal injection of a death row inmate are entirely intentional, but since they are justified under the law, it is not murder. Likewise, if one accidentally kills another person, while the act may still be criminal, as in a negligent homicide or manslaughter, it will not rise to the level of murder unless there is an intention to kill or at least a reckless disregard for human life. Today many jurisdictions divide murder by degrees. The most common divisions are between first and second-degree murder. Generally, first-degree murder is one that occurs after "premeditation, cool deliberation and planning," while second-degree murder is committed at the spur of the moment in the "heat of passion."

The Concept of Self-Defense

The right to defend oneself against an unwarranted attack is also an almost universally accepted concept. A person is always justified in the use of reasonable, non-deadly force to ward off an unwarranted attack. Typically, deadly force is only considered justified in cases where "the actor reasonably fears imminent peril of death or serious bodily harm to himself or another." From a legal perspective, the right to defend oneself provides a justification for an act of violence that would otherwise be criminal in and of itself. Thus, the right of self-defense is the right to use physical force to defend one's own life or the lives of others, including the use of deadly force.

This is distinguished from the right to defend one's property, which includes the right to use reasonable physical force, but excludes the right to use deadly force. Deadly force is generally defined as that degree of force that would be reasonably calculated to lead to death or serious bodily harm.

Interestingly, early theories made no distinction between the defense of the person and the defense of property. This was true in ancient Rome and in Old England where deadly force was allowed to protect mere property. All modern societies now recognize some distinction between defending property and defending life, namely that deadly force cannot be used to defend property.

To illustrate this distinction, imagine you are sleeping in a hotel when your car alarm wakes you in the night. As you pull open the curtains, you see that an assailant has broken into your vehicle and is stealing items from within. Despite the violation of personal property, since you are not in any physical danger, you are not legally allowed to pull open the window, draw a weapon and shoot the assailant (deadly force). You are allowed to confront the assailant and use reasonable force to stop the theft and/or to pursue and retrieve your personal property. If in doing so, the assailant draws a knife, the situation would then have escalated such that deadly force might be appropriate, depending upon whether you had a duty to retreat.

The Duty to Retreat

In many states there is a duty to retreat that must be observed before deadly force can be employed. It is usually articulated that, "deadly force may only be used if the person is unable to safely retreat from the confrontation." The duty to retreat is an additional component, which must be addressed if a defendant is to prove that his or her conduct in using deadly force was justified. In those jurisdictions where the requirement exists, the burden of proof is on the defendant to show that he was acting reasonably and could not have safely retreated from the confrontation, before eventually using deadly force.

The duty to retreat is not universal, however. For example, police officers are not required to retreat when acting in the line of duty. Similarly, some courts have found no duty to retreat exists when a victim is assaulted in his own home or in a place where he or she has a right to be.

A Representative Statute

Each state differs in regard to its self-defense laws. By way of example, the Florida statutes dealing with the justifiable use of force are summarized below. These laws incorporate all of the concepts discussed above in a succinct codified statute.

776.012 & .013 Use of force in defense of person.—A person is justified in using force, except deadly force, against another when and to the extent that the person reasonably believes that such conduct is necessary to defend himself or herself or another against the other's imminent use of unlawful force.

776.013 Use of Deadly Force.—A person is justified in the use of deadly force and does not have a duty to retreat if:

1. He or she reasonably believes that such force is necessary to prevent imminent death or great bodily harm to himself or herself or another or to prevent the imminent commission of a forcible felony; or

2. The person against whom the defensive force was used was in the process of unlawfully and forcefully entering, or had unlawfully and forcibly entered, a dwelling, residence, or occupied vehicle (note: there are exceptions to this rule for other residents, tenants and law enforcement officers entering homes in the line of duty).

776.013 Stand Your Ground.—A person who is not engaged in an unlawful activity and who is attacked in any other place where he or she has a right to be, has no duty to retreat and has the right to stand his or her ground and meet force with force, including deadly force, if he or she reasonably believes it is necessary to do so to prevent death or great bodily harm to himself or herself or another or to prevent the commission of a forcible felony.

776.041 Use of force by aggressor.—The justification described in the preceding sections of this chapter is not available to a person who:

1. is engaged in criminal activity or

2. initially provokes the use of force against himself or herself, unless he or she then exhausts every reasonable means to escape such danger.

"Make My Day Laws"

The concepts of the castle doctrine and stand-your-ground laws have been blended together in popular culture under the term "Make My Day Laws" which is a reference to the line "Go ahead, make my day," uttered by actor Clint Eastwood's character Harry Callahan in the 1983 film *Sudden Impact*, inviting a suspect to make himself liable to deadly retaliation by attacking Callahan. The film, as well as current events, have rekindled the debate as to whether the underlying purpose of these laws is being met.

The laws' effect on crime rates is disputed between supporters and critics of the laws. The third edition of *More Guns, Less Crime* by John Lott provides the most recent academic study on these laws. The research shows that states adopting "stand-your-ground" or "castle doctrine" laws saw murder rates reduced by 9 percent and overall violent crime by 11 percent. Florida State Representative Dennis Baxley, an author of the law in Florida, notes that crime rates in that state dropped significantly between 2005, when the law was passed, and 2012. These laws do have their critics. In a 2007 National District Attorneys Association symposium, numerous concerns were voiced that the law could increase crime, would allow criminals to use the law as a defense to their crimes, would result in more people carrying guns, could involve the misinterpretation of clues that could result in the use of deadly force when there was, in fact, no danger, and that racial and ethnic minorities would be at greater risk because of negative stereotypes. The George Zimmerman/Trayvon Martin case is a perfect example of the legitimacy of arguments on both sides of the issue.

The Best Rule of Thumb

Ultimately, whether you are a proponent of these laws or not, it is apparent that they have very deep roots in global jurisprudence, including here in the United States. The state-by-state application of the laws makes every case hinge on the specific facts to determine whether circumstances exist that allow for the use of deadly force. With every state having a different set of laws on the books, and each with various caveats and exceptions, it makes it impossible to opine any universal rule as to self-defense. Therefore, the best rule of thumb is that you can always use reasonable non-deadly force to defend yourself, your property and others, and you can use deadly force to protect yourself in your own home, but once outside the confines of your residence, one should seek all avenues to avoid any seriously escalated confrontation and only use deadly force if absolutely necessary.

Periodical and Internet Sources Bibliography

The following articles have been selected to supplement the diverse views presented in this chapter.

Dennis Baxley	"Op-Ed: Why I Wrote 'Stand Your Ground' Law," *Talk of the Nation*, National Public Radio, March 26, 2012. www.npr.org.
Clayton E. Cramer	"Domestic Violence & Stand Your Ground Laws," *Shotgun News*, June 1, 2012.
Peter Ferrara	"Stand Your Ground, Post-Trayvon Martin America, You're Not Racist," *Somewhat Reasonable* (blog), Heartland Institute, July 25, 2013. http://heartland.org.
Erica Goode	"N.R.A.'s Influence Seen in Expansion of Self-Defense Laws," *New York Times*, April 12, 2012.
Doug Howlett	"Has the Trayvon Martin Case Impacted Society's View of Guns?," *Guns & Ammo*, April 23, 2012.
Trymaine Lee	"Minister: Latest Teen Murder Shows Stand Your Ground 'Reeks of Racism,'" MSNBC, November 29, 2012. www.msnbc.com.
Tim Lynch	"Stand Your Ground Not Responsible for Trayvon Martin's Death," *Jurist*, April 6, 2012.
Elizabeth Schulte	"These Laws Stand for Racism," *Socialist Worker*, July 22, 2013.
Tampa Bay (FL) Times	"Repeal 'Stand Your Ground,'" June 10, 2012.
The Week	"Stand Your Ground Laws: Do They Offer a License to Kill?," April 27, 2012.
Adam Weinstein	"License to Kill: Immunity for Stand Your Ground Shooters," *Mother Jones*, July–August 2012.

For Further Discussion

Chapter 1

1. Victor E. Kappeler and Larry K. Gaines assert that community policing is misunderstood despite its successes. In your view, does their assertion make their definition of community policing biased? Why or why not?

2. Linda S. Miller, Kären Matison Hess, and Christine Hess Orthmann state that community involvement is important to community policing and explain how citizens participate. David Thacher maintains that community policing is not possible without the police. In your opinion, who plays the more important role in community policing? Use examples from the texts to explain your response.

3. William J. Harvey contends that community policing in practice is merely a program, and like most government-sponsored programs is temporary and disappears when federal funding is cut off. Considering the other viewpoints in the chapter, do you agree or disagree with the author? Explain.

Chapter 2

1. *Police* magazine offers several examples of success to support its argument of the effectiveness of community policing. Jeremy M. Wilson and Amy G. Cox performed their own analysis, however, and conclude that community policing may be ineffective. In your opinion, who provides the more persuasive argument? Cite examples from the viewpoints to support your answer.

Chapter 3

1. Sudhir Venkatesh insists that, despite their high numbers of arrests and convictions, federal agents undermine com-

munity policing because they do not mediate directly with criminals as local cops do. In your opinion, is mediation with criminals more important than arrests and convictions? Why or why not?

2. Chris Smith advocates the adoption of social services in community policing to reach at-risk youth. Dan Alexander suggests that social media technologies can help police better serve and engage with communities. In your view, which is better suited for the aims of community policing? Use examples from the texts to explain your response.

3. John Markovic insists that situational policing—responding to the unique needs and characteristics of neighborhoods—is relatively new and unproven, but will improve community policing. In your opinion, should situational policing be adopted regardless of being unfamiliar? Why or why not?

Chapter 4

1. Chris Kromm alleges that Stand Your Ground is a legal concept that promotes vigilantism based on suspicions and race. Does Robert VerBruggen successfully counter Kromm's allegation? Use examples from the text to explain your response.

Organizations to Contact

The editors have compiled the following list of organizations concerned with the issues debated in this book. The descriptions are derived from materials provided by the organizations. All have publications or information available for interested readers. The list was compiled on the date of publication of the present volume; the information provided here may change. Be aware that many organizations take several weeks or longer to respond to inquiries, so allow as much time as possible.

American Legislative Exchange Council (ALEC)

2900 Crystal Drive, 6th Floor, Arlington, VA   22202
(703) 373-0933 • fax: (703) 373-0927

ALEC works to advance the fundamental principles of free-market enterprise, limited government, and federalism at the state level through a nonpartisan public-private partnership of America's state legislators, members of the private sector, and the general public. The council advocates Stand Your Ground laws, incorporating Florida's law into its model legislation after it was enacted. On its website, ALEC provides its initiatives and model legislation on issues such as crime, criminal justice, and community safety.

Center for Problem-Oriented Policing (POP)

website: www.popcenter.org

Funded by the Office of Community Oriented Policing Services (COPS) of the US Justice Department, POP aims to advance the concept and practice of problem-oriented policing in open and democratic societies, offering accessible information about ways in which police can address specific crime and disorder problems. On its website, POP provides guides and publications on problem-oriented policing methods and on implementation, crime, and social disorder.

Justice Policy Institute (JPI)

1012 Fourteenth Street NW, Suite 400
Washington, DC   20005
(202) 558-7974 • fax: (202) 558-7978
website: www.justicepolicy.org

The mission of JPI is to reduce the use of incarceration and the justice system and promote policies that improve the well-being of all people and communities. The institute researches and analyzes programs and policies, disseminating its findings to the media, policy makers, and advocates while providing training and technical assistance support to people working for justice reform. JPI advocates alternatives to community policing, offering fact sheets and reports on issues related to law enforcement and criminal justice.

National Association of Police Organizations (NAPO)

317 S. Patrick Street, Alexandria, VA   22314-3501
(703) 549-0775 • fax: (703) 684-0515
e-mail: info@napo.org
website: www.napo.org

Founded in 1987, NAPO is a coalition of police unions and associations from across the United States that serves to advance the interests of America's law enforcement officers through legislative and legal advocacy, political action, and education. NAPO represents more than two thousand police units and associations, 241,000 sworn law enforcement officers, eleven thousand retired officers, and more than a hundred thousand citizen members. Its website offers commentary and articles on law enforcement, booklets on law enforcement legislation, and congressional testimony.

National Rifle Association (NRA)

11250 Waples Mill Road, Fairfax, VA   22030
(800) 672-3888
website: http://nra.org

Founded in 1871 to "promote and encourage rifle shooting on a scientific basis," the NRA advocates gun ownership under the Second Amendment as well as firearms education and training, marksmanship, and self-defense. The association also supports Stand Your Ground laws to protect personal safety. It publishes the journals *American Rifleman, American Hunter,* and *America's 1st Freedom.* The NRA website has a searchable archive that includes material such as congressional testimony about self-defense laws, NRA position papers, and video clips on the Barack Obama administration's stance on self-defense and home protection.

National Sheriffs' Association

1450 Duke Street, Alexandria, VA   22314-3490
(800) 424-7827 • fax: (703) 838-5349
www.sheriffs.org

Chartered in 1940, the National Sheriffs' Association is a professional organization dedicated to serving the office of sheriff and its affiliates through police education, police training, and general law enforcement information resources. The association represents thousands of sheriffs, deputies, and other law enforcement officers; public safety professionals; and concerned citizens nationwide. In 1972, the association established the National Neighborhood Watch Program in response to increasing crime. The group publishes *Sheriff* and *Deputy and Court Officer* magazines and the e-newsletter *NSA Capitol Watch.*

Office of Community Oriented Policing Services (COPS)

145 N Street NE, Washington, DC   20530
(800) 421-6770
e-mail: askcopsrc@usdoj.gov
website: www.cops.usdoj.gov

Established in 1994, COPS is the office of the US Department of Justice that advances the practice of community policing in America's state, local, and tribal law enforcement agencies. COPS does its work principally by sharing information and making grants to police departments around the United States. The office publishes an e-newsletter, *Community Policing Dispatch,* and offers other publications and resources on its website.

US Department of Justice (DOJ)

950 Pennsylvania Ave. NW, Washington, DC 20530-0001
(202) 514-2000
e-mail: askdoj@usdoj.gov
website: www.usdoj.gov

The mission of the DOJ is to enforce the law and defend the interests of the United States according to the law; to ensure public safety against threats foreign and domestic; to provide federal leadership in preventing and controlling crime; to seek just punishment for those guilty of unlawful behavior; and to ensure fair and impartial administration of justice for all Americans. The DOJ website provides various resources, including publications, reports, and legal briefs.

Bibliography of Books

Radley Balko

Rise of the Warrior Cop: The Militarization of America's Police Forces. New York: PublicAffairs, 2013.

Anthony A. Braga and David L. Weisburd

Policing Problem Places: Crime Hot Spots and Effective Prevention. New York: Oxford University Press, 2010.

Andrew F. Branca

The Law of Self Defense: The Indispensable Guide to the Armed Citizen. 2nd ed. Maynard, MA: Law of Self Defense, 2013.

Lee P. Brown

Policing in the 21st Century: Community Policing. Bloomington, IN: AuthorHouse, 2012.

Jake V. Burke, ed.

Community Oriented Policing: Background and Issues. New York: Nova Science, 2010.

Jeremy G. Carter

Intelligence-Led Policing: A Policing Innovation. El Paso, TX: LFB Scholarly, 2013.

James J. Chriss

Beyond Community Policing: From Early American Beginnings to the 21st Century. Boulder, CO: Paradigm, 2013.

James A. Conser, Rebecca Paynich, and Terry Gingerich

Law Enforcement in the United States. 3rd ed. Burlington, MA: Jones & Bartlett, 2013.

John S. Dempsey and Linda S. Forst	*An Introduction to Policing.* Clifton Park, NY: Delmar/Cengage Learning, 2013.
Peter Grabosky, ed.	*Community Policing and Peacekeeping.* Boca Raton, FL: CRC Press, 2009.
Heath B. Grant and Karen J. Terry	*Law Enforcement in the 21st Century.* Boston: Pearson, 2012.
Nathan F. Iannone, Marvin D. Iannone, and Jeff Bernstein	*Supervision of Police Personnel.* 8th ed. Boston: Pearson, 2014.
Charles McNeeley	*Community Policing: Building Inclusive Communities.* Jackson, MS: Lamar, 2006.
Veerendra Mishra	*Community Policing: Misnomer or Fact?* Thousand Oaks, CA: Sage, 2011.
Michael J. Palmiotto	*Community Policing.* Sudbury, MA: Jones & Bartlett, 2006.
Kenneth J. Peak, Larry K. Gaines, and Ronald W. Glensor	*Police Supervision and Management: In an Era of Community Policing.* Upper Saddle River, NJ: Prentice Hall, 2010.
Kenneth J. Peak and Ronald W. Glensor	*Community Policing and Problem Solving: Strategies and Practices.* 6th ed. Boston: Pearson, 2012.

Sharon Pickering,   *Counter-terrorism Policing:*
Jude McCulloch,   *Community, Cohesion, and Security.*
and David Wright   New York: Springer, 2008.

M. Alper Sozer   *Crime and Community Policing.* El
Paso, TX: LFB Scholarly, 2009.

Norm Stamper   *Breaking Rank: A Top Cop's Exposé of
the Dark Side of American Policing.*
New York: Nation Books, 2005.

Charles R.   *Police Administration: Structures,*
Swanson, Leonard *Processes, and Behavior.* 8th ed.
Territo, and   Boston: Pearson, 2012.
Robert W. Taylor

Hans Toch and J.   *Police as Problem Solvers: How
Douglas Grant   Frontline Workers Can Promote
Organizational and Community
Change.* Washington, DC: American
Psychological Association, 2005.

Fritz Umbach   *The Last Neighborhood Cops: The Rise
and Fall of Community Policing in
New York Public Housing.* New
Brunswick, NJ: Rutgers University
Press, 2011.

Mitch Vilos and   *Self-Defense Laws of All 50 States.* 2nd
Evan Vilos   ed. Centerville, UT: Guns West, 2013.

Jeremy M. Wilson *Community Policing in America.* New
York: Routledge, 2006.

Index

A

Agreda, Erik, 120–121, 123
Alexander, Dan, 124–131
Alexander, Michelle, 90
Alliance of Guardian Angels, 37–38, 114
Al Qaeda, 54
American Border Patrol (ABP), 39
American Legislative Exchange Council, 162
American Prospect (magazine), 118
American Recovery and Reinvestment Act (2009), 102
Anomic neighborhoods, 137
Arab-American populations, 53, 56
Arlington (TX) Police Department, 40
Arrests
    citizen arrests, 37, 88
    citizen information on, 127
    by community policing officers, 24
    decrease in, 117
    FBI taskforce, 111
    high-profile, 113
    by law enforcement, 29, 30, 49, 114, 122
    Stand Your Ground laws and, 177
    of Zimmerman, George, 87–88, 92, 174, 176, 181
Assault
    duty to retreat and, 193
    of Martin, Trayvon, 87
    as not a crime, 174
protection from, 187
reduction in, 15
Stand Your Ground laws and, 178
Automobile thefts, 15

B

Barker, Thomas, 145
Baxley, Dennis, 186, 194
Bayley, David, 26
Beard v. United States (1895), 183–184, 188
Beat checks, 73
Bellevue (WA) Police Department, 42
Bensen, Mark, 186
Benson, Bruce, 70–71, 78
Billings (MT) Police Department, 43
Blockos (group), 38
Bloomberg, Michael, 181
Blow, Charles, 88
Boca Raton (FL) Police Services Department (BRPD), 125, 127, 128
Boise (ID) Police Department, 75
Bones, William L., 76
Bonilla-Silva, Eduardo, 162
Bottom-up thinking, 156
Brewster, JoAnne, 41
Brown, Peter A., 162
Brown v. Board of Education (1954), 90
Brown v. United States (1921), 183
Bucqueroux, Bonnie, 98–99, 154

Bureau of Justice Assistance, 42, 153, 155

Burglaries, 15, 31, 74, 165, 169

Bush, George W., administration, 62, 113

Bush, Jeb, 166

C

Call-and-response strategies, 19

Castle Doctrine, 166–169, 180–188

Church organizations, 47

Citizen arrests, 37, 88

Citizen Corps partner programs, 41

Citizen patrols, 37–39

Citizen volunteers, 41–43

Citizens' police academies (CPAs), 39–41

Civilian Complaint Review Board (CCRB), 35

Civilian oversight, 35–37

Clinton, Bill, administration, 61, 112, 114

Combee, Neil, 179

Community Action Officer (CAO), 74

Community involvement
    as alternative to police, 47–48
    balance with police, 37
    citizen patrols, 37–39
    citizen volunteers, 41–43
    citizens' police academies, 39–41
    civilian oversight, 35–37
    civilian review boards, 35
    community policing and, 33–43
    overview, 34–35

Community Oriented Police Enforcement (COPE), 70, 78

Community Oriented Policing Services (COPS)
    budget cuts to, 101
    funding for, 102, 107, 112
    Hiring Program, 15
    introduction, 14–15
    problem-oriented policing approach, 20
    public's expectations, 27

Community policing
    arrests, 30
    components, 23–25
    confusion over, 25–27
    democratic management style, 156
    full-time use of, *23*
    investigations, 30–31
    overviews, 14–17, 19–20, 22–23
    planning and implementation, 148–159
    police participation in, 44–51
    police-community relations, 140–147
    politics and, 105–106
    preservation strategies, 106–109
    as problem solving, 21–27
    rapid response, 29–30
    routine patrols, 29
    social media and, 124–131
    social services and, 64, 115–123
    traditional policing differences, 29–32
    training in, 14, 98–99, 146
    truth of, 60–64
    waning nature of, 63

See also Community involvement; Law enforcers/enforcement

Community policing, effectiveness
country *vs.* city, 73
crime rates and, 80–85
geographical considerations, 75–76
good cops and, 77
if properly practiced, 69–79
individual initiative and, 70–71
manpower issues, 77–78
overview, 67–68, 70
problems with, 76
public relations and, 78–79
traditional policing compared to, 71–72

Community policing, improvements needed
community needs, 132–139
community relationships, 102–103
federal support concerns, 109–114
media relationships, 103–104
neighborhood types, 135–137
support needs, 100–108

Community Policing Advisory Board, 122

Community Policing Committee (IACP), 56

Comprehensive School Safety Program, 15

Conceal carry laws, 167

Conflicted neighborhoods, 138

Conflict resolution, 46

Conti, Norman, 134–135

Cordero, Michael A., 63

Cox, Amy G., 80–85

CQ Press, 118

Crank, John P., 63

Crime-prevention efforts
beat officers, 119
citizenship role in, 16, 87
community-based, 50
community policing and, 26, 74–76
federal taskforces, 112
goals, 144
information sharing in, 31
outreach teams, 122
PSO program, 82
VIPER branding, 126
See also National Neighborhood Watch Program

Crime rates
in anomic neighborhoods, 137
community-oriented policing and, 71
decrease, 187–188
hiring grants impact, 16
Make My Day laws and, 194
National Neighborhood Watch Program and, 67
problem-solving officer program and, 82

D

Davis, Jordan, 179

Deadly force
best rule of thumb for, 195
concept of murder, 191
concept of self-defense, 191–192
duty to retreat, 192–193
Make My Day laws, 194–195
overview, 190
self-defense laws, 193–194
in Stand Your Ground laws, 189–195

Dearborn (MI) Police Department, 53–55
Decentralized police service, 24
Defining the Community in Community Policing (Flynn), 133
De Jesus, Miguel, 165
DeLord, Ron, 72, 78
DelToro, Anthony, 116–117
Democratic management style, 156
Dependent neighborhoods, 137–138
Disorderly behavior, 45–46
Door-to-door visits, 26
Drug Enforcement Administration (DEA), 111
Dunn, Michael, 179
Duty to retreat, 186, 192–193

E

Eck, John E., 19
England, 50, 58, 88, 89, 181, 192
Evans, William N., 15–16

F

Facebook, 125, 127
Fairlawn Coalition, 38
Federal Bureau of Investigation (FBI), 110–111, 114
Ferrara, Joe, 104
Flint (MI) Police Department, 70–71, 78
Florida Prosecuting Attorneys Association, 168
Flynn, Daniel W., 133
Foot patrols, 25–26
Foster, Janet, 50–51
Freeman-Otte, Katherine, 140–147

Friedmann, Robert, 56–58
Friend, Zach, 100–108

G

Gaines, Larry K., 21–27
Gangs/gang members, 31, 40, 111, 118
Garland, David, 88
Georgetown Public Policy Institute, 104
Ghost Town neighborhood (West Oakland, CA), 122
Goffman, Erving, 49–50
Goldstein, Herman, 19
Grabosky, Peter, 48
Grant, Kevin, 117, 122
Great Britain. *See* England
Guardian Angels. *See* Alliance of Guardian Angels

H

Hammer, Marion, 167–168
Hanna, Joe, 95
Harcourt, Bernard, 47–48, 50
Harvey, William L., 60–64
Hate crimes, 53
Havis, Devonya N., 178
Heritage Foundation's Center for Data Analysis (CDA), 16
Hess, Kären Matison, 33–43
Hewitt, Christina, 93
High-profile arrests, 113
Hiring grants, 14–16
Holmes, Oliver Wendell, 184–185
Homeland security
    funding for, 62
    overview, 52–55
    role of, 57–59

Homicide
  concept, 191
  investigations, 40
  justifiable, 166–167, 181–182
  reductions, 15, 71
Horn, Joe, 165, 169
Huberman, Ron, 130
Human Rights Watch, 53
Hunter, Ronald D., 145

I

Immigration and Customs Enforcement (ICE), 111
Interdependent neighborhoods, 138
International Association of Chiefs of Police (IACP), 41, 56
Investigations, 30–31

J

Jackson, Jesse, 181, 187
Jacobsen, R.C. (Jake), 73–75
Jaywalkers, 49
Jim Crow laws, 89–90
John Jay College of Criminal Justice, 117
Jones, Will, 183
Jordan, Howard, 119, 122, 123
Journal of Homeland Security and Emergency Management, 58
Justifiable homicides, 166–167, 181–182
Juvenile crimes, 40

K

Kappeler, Victor E., 21–27
Kennedy, David, 117–118
Kerns, Jim, 76

Kind, Adam, 185–187
Kolb, Nancy, 42
Kovandzic, Tom, 16
Kromm, Chris, 164–170
Kuykendall, J.L., 155

L

Law Enforcement Association of Texas (CLEAT), 72, 78
Law enforcers/enforcement
  arrests by, 29, 30, 49, 114, 122
  civilian review boards and, 35–37
  disorder and, 48–49
  disorder management by, 49–51
  information sharing, 32
  involvement in community policing, 31, 44–51
  local law enforcement, 15, 112
  National Neighborhood Watch Programs, 88–90, *89*
  no monopoly on security, 40
  overview, 45–47
  police mission, 22, 29–30
  as political, 105–106
  role, 22
  situational police styles, *134*, 134–135, 138–139
  social services, 120
  See also Community policing
Legal killing with vigilantism, 168–170
Lethal injection, 191
Lifeline program, 117–122
Link, Don, 122
Local law enforcement, 15, 112
Long Island University, 58
Lott, John, 162–163, 194

Lott, Sherwin, 162–163
Love, Dwayne, 31

M

Make My Day laws, 194–195
Markovic, John, 132–139
Martin, Trayvon
  deadly force controversy, 190,
    195
  Neighborhood Watch Groups
    and, 87–88, 90, 92
  shooting of, 172–174, 176, 179
  Stand Your Ground laws and,
    162, 181, 185
  vigilantism and, 164–170
Martinez, Rick, 100–108
Mathews, Cynthia, 102, 104, 105
Matthews, Roger, 47, 50
McDevitt, Jack, 134–135
McDonald, Barbara, 130
Measure Y. See Violence Preven-
  tion and Public Safety Act
  (2004)
Media relationships, 103–104
Michigan State University School
  of Criminal Justice, 71
Miller, Linda S., 33–43
Miller, Mary, 102–103
More Guns, Less Crime (Lott), 194
Morrison, Bo, 185–187
Muhlhausen, David B., 16
Murder. See Homicide
Muslims, 53

N

National Crime Prevention Survey,
  67

National District Attorneys Association, 168, 194–195
National Institute of Justice, 156
National Neighborhood Watch
  Program
  establishment, 67
  fear of crime and, 90
  idea of, 26, 93–94
  increased safety concerns,
    86–90
  intangible benefits, 94–95
  law enforcement through, 88–
    90, 89
  no police powers, 94
  overview, 87–88, 92–93
  should not be armed, 91–95
National Network for Safe Com-
  munities (NNSC), 118
National Rifle Association (NRA),
  167, 168
National Sheriffs' Association, 67,
  87, 92, 94
Nation of Islam, 38
Naval Postgraduate School's Cen-
  ter for Homeland Defense and
  Security, 58
Neighborhood Contact Officer
  (NCO), 70, 75
Neighborhood Enforcement Team
  (NET), 74
Neighborhood Oriented Policing
  (NOP), 72
Neighborhood Service Team
  (NST), 75
Neighborhoods
  anomic neighborhoods, 137
  Arab-American neighbor-
    hoods, 56
  community responsibility for,
    76, 102, 106, 120, 157

conflicted neighborhoods, 138
dependent neighborhoods,
137–138
interdependent neighbor-
hoods, 138
needs, 133–136, *134*
patrols in, 39, 67, 92–93
police programs for, 75, 143
problem-solving in, 139
responsive neighborhoods,
137
rough/troubled neighbor-
hoods, 116–117, 187
stages, 137–138
strong neighborhoods, 136
types, 135–137
vulnerable neighborhoods,
136
New York Times (newspaper), 38,
88, 168
New Zealand, 48
Nicholl, Caroline G., 40
Nieves, Ted, 77–78
9/11 attacks. *See* September 11,
2001, attacks
Noise pollution, 45
Nolan, James, 134–135, 136, 137
Noncoercive interventions, 49
Norteño gang neighborhood, 116
Novak, Kenneth J., 93–94, 95

O

Oakland (CA) Police Department
(OPD), 80–85, 119
Obama, Barack, administration,
113
Office of Justice Programs, 42
Online reporting systems, 30
Operation Ceasefire, 118
Orlando Sentinel (newspaper), 179

Orthmann, Christine Hess, 33–43
Ortiz, Diego, 165
Owens, Emily G., 15–16

P

Page, Douglas, 52–59
Palm Beach (FL) Police Depart-
ment, 41
Palmiotto, Michael J., 148–159
Paramilitary organizations, 147
Park keepers, 47
Parks, Rosa, 181
Peaden, Durell, 169
Peaslee, Liliokanaio, 120
Peters, Justin, 175–179
Phoenix (AZ) Law Enforcement
Association, 73
Phoenix (AZ) Police Department,
73–75
Physical coercion, 48
Planning and implementation of
community policing
defined, 150–151
overview, 149–150
personnel for, 155–157
reasons for, 151–153
Police. *See* Law enforcers/
enforcement
Police (magazine), 69–79
Police academy training, 31, 98
Police training officer (PTO) pro-
gram, 106
Police-community relations
community policing and, 140–
147
connection and communica-
tion, 143–144
contrasts in, 144–145
failures of, 146–147

meaning, 141–142

overview, 141

public relations and, 142–145, 143*t*

Posse comitatus powers, 88

Priority Estates Project, 50

Problem-oriented policing (POP)

analysis of, 82–83

crime reduction from, 80–85

implementation challenges, 84

overview, 19–20, 27, 81

policy implications, 84–85

progress with, 82

statistics, 83

Problem-solving officer (PSO) program, 81–82

Public information officer (PIO), 104, 127, 130–131

Public order, 45–47, 50

Public relations efforts, 26, 78–79, 144

Public safety outcomes

arrests and, 30

funding for, 107

importance, 47, 104–105

improvements, 15, 41, 133

incarcerations and, 114

police monopoly on, 40

responsibility for, 102, 110, 112

Stand Your Ground laws and, 181

support for, 137

Public urination, 45, 50

Public relations *vs.* community relations, 142–145, 143*t*

Q

Quality-of-life issues, 22, 75

Quick Response (QR) codes, 125

Quinnipiac University, 162

R

Racism and criminal justice, 87–88

Racism Without Racists: Color-Blind Racism and the Persistence of Racial Inequality in America (Bonilla-Silva), 162

Rapid response, 29–30

Reaves, Brian A., 25

Recidivism rates, 122

Repeat offenders, 30, 120

Responsive neighborhoods, 137

Reyes, Kris, 103

Robberies, 15–16, 40

Roberts, Joshua K., 189–195

Rogers, Steven L., 77

Roman, John, 162

Rosenbaum, Dennis, 93

Routine patrols, 29, 69

Rubinkam, Michael, 91–95

S

Safe Streets Taskforce, 111

San Diego (CA) Police Department, 42

Santa Cruz (CA) Police Department, 101, 103, 107

Santa Cruz Neighbors (organization), 102

Scanning, Analysis, Response, and Assessment (SARA) model, 19

Scheider, Matthew, 28–32

Scott, Rick, 176
Segura, Liliana, 165
Self-defense
    concept, 191–192
    statutes, 169, 184, 193–194
    Stand Your Ground laws and,
        177–178
Sennett, Richard, 46–47
September 11, 2001, attacks, 55–56
Sharpton, Al, 181, 187
Silverman, E., 152
Simon, Jonathan, 86–90
Situational police styles, *134*, 134–
    135, 138–139
Sliwa, Curtis, 37
Sloan, Ron, 98–99
Smith, Chris, 115–123
Social media
    benefits *vs.* costs, 131
    community policing and, 124–
        131
    defined goals and, 126–128
    overcoming obstacles with,
        128–131
    overview, 124–126
Social services, 64, 115–123
Sparrow, Malcolm, 149–150
Spelman, William, 19
Stand Your Ground (SYG) laws
    cases, 178–179
    Castle Doctrine and, 166–169,
        180–188
    dangers, 171–174
    deadly force and, 189–195
    debate over, 88
    duty to retreat and, 186
    lobbyist for, 167–168
    overview, 162–163
    put safety at risk, 175–179
    self-defense *vs.*, 177–178
    statutes, 193–194

True Man Doctrine and, 182–
    183
    vigilantism promoted by, 164–
        170
State law enforcement, 15
State-of-the-art training, 15
Station guards, 47
Storey, Stephanie, 169
Street Outreach team, 116–117
Strong neighborhoods, 136
Subway fare beating, 48
Sudden Impact (film), 194
Suffolk County (NY) Police De-
    partment, 77–78
Supinski, Stanley, 58–59

T

Tampa Bay Times (newspaper),
    166
Teen Police Academy, 41
Thatcher, David, 44–51
Theft. *See* Burglaries
Till, Emmet, 90
Trade union associations, 47
Traditional policing
    basic beliefs of, 27
    community empowerment
        and, 22
    community policing *vs.*, 28–32
    as core, 32
    transition from, 150
Training in community policing,
    14, 98–99, 146
Tribal law enforcement, 15
Trojanowicz, Robert C., 98, 154
True Man Doctrine, 182–183,
    186–187
Tutko, Chris, 92, 94